ISSUES WHITE-ANTING INDIA

As an NRI sees it

ISSUES WHITE-ANTING INDIA

As an NRI sees it

Bill K Koul

Vitasta
LET KNOWLEDGE SPREAD

Published by
Renu Kaul Verma
Vitasta Publishing Pvt Ltd
2/15, Ansari Road, Daryaganj
New Delhi - 110 002
info@vitastapublishing.com

ISBN 978-93-86473-13-4

Cover and layout by Vits Press
Printed by Vikas Computer and Printers

To Rani, my mother, who gave me birth, nourished me, brought me up and gave me the essential values of life

&

To my Mother India, where I was born and where I grew up and where I received my education

&

To all my teachers in India, past and present, young and old, who taught me, in their own unique ways, the meaning of life, how to live and what to live for

&

Most importantly, this book is dedicated to the youth of India and their future generations.

I thank you all for inspiring me to write this book.

Foreword

I was born and raised in India. Since 1995, I have been mainly living outside my mother country but my roots are very much entrenched there. I pay her a short visit a number of times every year to catch up with my family and friends. Sadly, with each trip, I find it is increasingly difficult and challenging to live a healthy life in India and come out without falling sick. The problem is that these challenges have not remained constant with time; they seem to be increasing with each day.

After their arrival in India, most tourists, whether they are Overseas Citizens of India (OCI) like me, or Non Resident Indians (NRI), or foreigners—face similar issues and challenges immediately after their arrival and during their stay in India, which are distinctly and uniquely Indian.

It would be reasonable to consider the experience of a regular visitor to the country, like me and millions like me, as a barometer of the country's health.

This book raises many ground issues that need urgent attention by all people and stakeholders in India for the sake of their children and all future generations. If something is not done now to address these issues, the country may potentially choke itself in the next couple of decades or so. Unfortunately, a painful realisation is that, in general, many people in India seem to be sleepwalking through these issues.

While making such assertions, I am cognisant of the fact that, as I am growing older, I am also growing a shade more impatient with each visit. However, notwithstanding that, with each year India is becoming (a) more populated; (b) more polluted; and (c) hotter. Therefore, there is no dispute to the claim that life in India is becoming increasingly difficult and unhealthy with each passing day.

I am also cognisant of the fact, and feel as proud as the rest of my Indian community, about the outstanding progress that the country has made in the last seven decades since her independence. I can even write a book or two highlighting those achievements. But, at this point of time, I am more concerned about the future of her children and their children.

My immediate concern is that I want to be able to visit my motherland 20 years from now. However, going by the direction in which overall living conditions and the environment in India seems to be heading at present, it seems unlikely that I could visit her at all after two decades from now. It is not that I will not be able to afford the airfare, or I would be too old or unhealthy or weak to travel, but because the country may not be habitable at all at that time.

What I am going to summarise in this book may not please many readers in India. Many may consider it rather offensive and completely unacceptable: some due to their pride as individuals, which is quite justified; some due to their nationalism, which is also justified; but an overwhelming majority purely due to their selfish and thoughtless consumerism, materialism and corruption, ignorance and devil-may-care attitude, which cannot be justified.

The book is based on my personal observations and understanding of some real life events during my visits to India in 2016 and 2017, and my interaction with a number of people in Bombay, New Delhi and Jammu. For correlation and comparison purposes, reference has also been made to my observations of life in India, pre-1995, and my life outside India.

This book has six chapters. Chapter 1 identifies and discusses various serious social issues, as I see and understand them, and how they potentially white-ant the life in the country. Chapters 2 to 5 provide various vignettes based on my visits to India during the months of summer (July 2016), autumn (November 2016), winter (December 2016) and spring (March 2017). These vignettes have actually inspired me to write this book; Chapter 6 provides a summary of the way forward, as I see it.

My appeal to all fellow Indians, for the sake of the health and survival of our motherland is: Immediately stop increasing your population, consume fewer natural resources, eat sensibly and healthily, relearn to live a simpler and more spiritual life, live in harmony and peace with one another, and work hard for your country. You must preserve the country and her natural resources for the future generations—you owe it to them. Like termites and cancer cells, you must not devour everything that comes your way. The country's Prime Minister, Mr Narendra Modi, is a great role model for you to follow—for his simplicity, sincerity, dedication and hard work. You are lucky to have him as your leader; this is your chance to redeem yourselves.

As a practicing engineer, I follow the "KISS" rule (acronym used in the engineering industry for 'keep it simple and stupid'). It is possible that I may have oversimplified certain complex human psychological and social issues in this book.

The readers are, however, free to disagree with my understandings and interpretations based on their own individual experiences and understanding of such matters. In the civilised world, don't we follow the '*freedom of expression and speech*' approach to deal with issues in life?

My final cry is: Please put a solid lid on your population. Stop producing more, at least for next five to ten years. Bring the country's birth rate below her death rate, so that the net population growth is negative for a decade or so. Mother India can't breastfeed any more people. She is struggling; she may die. She is crying through her sons, like me, and millions like me living in India; please listen to us.

Author's Note

You may ask about my credibility in raising a number of serious and sensitive social and life issues in this book. Am I a social worker or a social scientist, or a politician, or an academic, or a philosopher, or an emancipated spiritual guru? No, I am none of these.

I am currently a practicing professional engineer, a Fellow of Engineers Australia. In Australia, I am a registered Chartered Professional Engineer, with registration in the APEC countries. I am also an Associate Fellow of Australian Institute of Management. In India, I am a life member of the Institution of Engineers (India), as well as the Indian Society of Technical Education.

My specialisation is civil-geotechnical engineering, which, in layman's language, means that I deal with the foundations of man-made structures constructed on the earth. My role is to ensure that structures that I deal with, such as buildings, bridges, railways, roads, towers, tunnels etc., are well supported from below, remain stable and don't collapse due to poor foundation conditions, during their design life.

It is logical that, based on my regular visits to India, and my close observations and rational thinking, coupled with my intellectual interactions with a range of fellow Indians through a wide cross-section of the Indian community, I feel extremely concerned and worried about the future of living conditions in India. I see her foundations infested with a number of serious and ground issues, many of which seem to be unnoticed but which seem to act as termites or white-ants, with the potential to undermine the foundation of the country itself. If the foundations of a structure are found to be infested with termites, one can consciously undertake an appropriate and effective anti-termite treatment to completely get rid of them. However, if the citizens of a country themselves act as termites, albeit unknowingly, what can one do?

I am conscious of the fact that many of my fellow Indians may totally dismiss the contents of this book on several pretexts. Some of them may say, "This guy lives in a foreign country—what does he know about India? He has just some shallow and superficial knowledge about India, and lacks a deeper understanding about the country and our culture. Let him live and work here and then talk." Well, that may or may not be correct. I would like to request all such people who claim to have a much deeper and broader understanding of the country to rise and do something about the problems. Making sweeping statements or dismissing others does not help anyone.

There may be others who may just make passing comments like, "*Chalta hai; yahan to aisa he hota hai; sub thheek ho jayega.* India is great!" ("This is how this country works; all will be well in due course. India is great!"). Well, I don't disagree with the last part of that comment. India has been and is a great country; no one can dispute that. But the days of saying "all will be well" seem to be well and truly numbered. Things can't keep on going for ever the way things are alarmingly shaping up on the horizon; people must wake up now and help their nation to help themselves.

I believe in simple and straight solutions and a direct approach to tackle problems and achieve tangible results within reasonable time frames. Anything that is not simple, or can't be simplified, cannot be considered to be sustainable and practical. For addressing critical and urgent issues, such as those raised in this book, I believe one must adopt an open and out-of-the-box, multi-faceted, approach, which is prudent and fearless, impartial, unbiased, sincere and direct. One must go to the root of those issues and analyse them threadbare, one by one. Thereafter, one must make noise about the issues, followed by thorough planning and a careful strategy to implement all effective, timely and appropriate solutions, through multi-pronged channels: both administrative and a direct nationwide campaign, including a door-to-door educational drive for the people of India by the people of India, and the relevant stakeholders, in a truly democratic way.

I was born and raised at Srinagar, in Kashmir. In early 1990, under duress, and along with 100,000 other Pandit families, our family moved to Jammu, the winter capital of Jammu & Kashmir.

As part of REC Srinagar (now NIT Srinagar), I lived and worked at Jammu from 1990 till the time I left India, with my young family, in early 1995. During that stint, I was a part of the core team from the REC which planned and set up the Government College of Engineering & Technology (GCET), Jammu, the first ever government engineering college at Jammu.

Jammu has played a significant role in the survival and settlement of nearly half a million Kashmiri Pandits after their unfortunate and sudden exodus from Kashmir in 1990, and the preservation of their traditions and culture. I sincerely acknowledge and thank the people of Jammu for their warm hospitality and sincere support. The people of Jammu showed an exemplary high degree of tolerance, goodwill and adaptability towards Kashmiri Pandits who brought an entirely different culture to the City of Temples in 1990.

My late grandfather, Pandit Shamboo Nath Koul, was an eminent educationist. For nearly five decades (1930s to 1970s), he enjoyed a great reputation in J & K as a teacher of Mathematics and English. He obtained his BA from Sri Pratap (SP) College in Srinagar and then his BT degree (Bachelor of Teaching, now BEd) from the Prince of Wales College, Jammu, now known as the Science College, Jammu.

Between 1951 and 1958, he taught Mathematics and English to the matriculation students at Sri Ranbir High School (SRHS), Jammu, in the august company of various esteemed and noted educationists of that time, such as Mr Niranjan Dass Suri, Mr Ram Lal Bargotra and Mr Tej Ram Khajuria. My family lived in a Custodian property, at House No 518, Peer Mitha, located in the downtown part of Jammu, at a monthly rent of Rupees 10, payable to the government. Interestingly, in 1958, the family completely left the possession of that property, which not many other people have ever done. In 2002, my parents built a house at Jammu, Hazuri Bagh (TalabTillo).

My father, Mr Jawahar Lal Koul (retired Chief Engineer, PWD Kashmir), completed his matriculation from SRHS, Jammu. Thereafter, he completed his BA degree from Amar Singh College at Srinagar. In 1965, he obtained his BSc (Eng) degree from Punjab Engineering College, Chandigarh. He lives currently at Jammu.

Acknowledgements

My eternal gratitude goes to my parents, Rani and Boba, and to my spiritual master, Baisahib (Bansi Lal Hakhu).

I sincerely thank my friend and a fellow meditator, Subash, who lives at Delhi, for his valuable input in Chapter 2 of this book. My sincere thanks also go to my other friends—Ashok Jain (Ground Engineering India, Delhi), Rakesh Misri (HPCL, Mumbai), Romesh Bhat (DLF, Delhi), Sunil Bhat (Doctor, Perth) and Rajinder Braroo (Jammu), for their interaction with me during 2016 and 2017. Without them, a number of vignettes presented in Chapters 2 to 4 of this book were not possible. My sincere thanks also go to my colleagues at Perth—Ian Lewis and Payam Sadeghi, and my philosopher friend, Dale Hartley (Blue Wheelers, Perth) for exchanging their thoughts with me. The idea of writing this book struck me during my visit to India in November 2016. At that time, I was in the midst of completing the manuscript of my second book, *My Life Does Not Have to Be Unhappy*. My first book, *Twenty Two Years*, is related to my exodus from Kashmir and my early life in the Kashmir valley.

I had to overcome a number of serious and challenging issues on several fronts, which had the potential to seriously undermine my efforts to be able to finish writing this book. I fondly remember my erstwhile teacher of Engineering Geology at REC Srinagar, Professor Parbin Singh, who was also later my colleague and the Coordinator at the REC Srinagar—Camp classes, Jammu. He once said, "*Whenever a positive and noble thought is born in your mind, be aware that an equivalent but negative thought will be born elsewhere at the same time to undermine your thought. So before that opposing thought reaches and overwhelms you, be quick to translate your positive thought into a meaningful action.*" Professor Singh was a man of action—sincere, wise, serene and thorough. My deep and heartfelt homage goes to him. May he rest in peace!

I thank all my family members for bearing with me during the writing of the book. My gratitude goes to Renu Kaul Verma of Vitasta Publishing for publishing this book; and my editor, Veena Batra, for her competent editing. I acknowledge their constructive comments and useful suggestions, and sincerely thank them both for shaping this book and bringing it to the readers in its final form.

Last, but not the least, I must sincerely thank *The Times of India* ("TOI") for raising numerous serious issues facing the country, such as the falling gender ratio, growing pollution, traffic woes, sexual assaults on women, corruption etc., from time to time. Many of the articles recently published by the TOI have provided timely support to me during the writing phase of this book, as if they were God sent. Thank you TOI.

How I wrote this book?

The idea of writing this book was born during a 10-day visit to India in Oct / Nov 2016, to catch up with my friends at Mumbai and Delhi, and to attend a family weeding at Jammu. Before flying to Jammu, I stayed at Mumbai for two days. Except for the usual humidity, I enjoyed my stay at Mumbai. My friend lives on Marine Drive. The area is usually quite breezy and relatively much cleaner than the suburbs. At Jammu, I found many people were suffering from seasonal health issues, such as cough and viral fever. At that time, Jammu had not received any rainfall for quite some time, so the dust and smoke levels were very high, and the suspended particulate matter in the air carried bacteria quickly from one person to the other. Normally, the Jammu air is much clearer than Delhi. A couple of days after the wedding, I also came down with low level fever, fatigue and a runny nose. With each day, my condition became worse. Two days before starting my return journey from Jammu, I started a course of antibiotics on the doctor's advice I needed a precautionary quick fix to control my symptoms before taking my international flight out of Delhi.

At noon of 4 November, I landed at Delhi. The visibility at the airport, and on the roads, was relatively much lower than normal, due to a smog that had been engulfing Delhi soon after the festival of Deepawali. Later it was found that the smog was due to a deliberate crop burning exercise in areas adjacent to Delhi. I was lucky that my flight was not cancelled or postponed, as had been happening on a regular basis at that time. Even the trains were running very late, some up to 24 hours. The whole environment in Delhi was very depressing, especially for a visitor like me. The early afternoon sun resembled a yellow moon, warm but dull. The Delhi residents seemed to be going about their business as usual. Although I felt sicker than before, I had to travel long distances in the national capital to meet various people. In the evening, I played badminton in an open air court with my friend, Mr Ashok Jain (my erstwhile employer in 1990), at his home in Green Park. The next morning, Mr Jain came down with fever, cough and a chest related issue. During the day, he and I went on a day-long, work-related trip within Delhi. During that trip, I wondered in disbelief how people lived and worked in Delhi. I was deeply worried about how Delhi would look like in the next 20 years. The idea of writing this book was born then.

In the evening, I flew out of Delhi and, thankfully, managed to reach Perth. I started writing this book on 25 November 2016.

When people don't listen, they must be given something to read and ponder over.

"*Raise your words, not voice. It is rain that grows flowers, not thunder.*" (Rumi)

Contents

Dedication *v*

Foreword *vii*

Author's Note *xi*

Acknowledgements *xv*

How I wrote this book? *xvii*

Chapter 1 White-anting Issues 1

1.0 INTRODUCTION 1

1.1 WHY THIS BOOK? 4

1.1.1 What Comprises a Healthy Living? 13

1.2 INDIA'S OUTSTANDING ACHIEVEMENTS 14

1.3 A DISTINCT INDIAN EXPERIENCE 18

1.3.1 A Familiar and Distinct Indian Odour ... 18

1.3.2 Immigration 19

1.3.3 Checked-in Baggage 20

1.3.4 Polluted Air 20

1.3.5 Transport & Traffic 22

1.3.6 Drinking Water 24

1.3.7 Fruits, Vegetables& Dairy products 25

1.3.8 Spurious and Fake Medicines 28

1.3.9 Superbugs 30
1.3.10 General Safety & Security Concerns 31
1.4 CORRUPTION & WHITE-ANTING ISSUES 32
1.5 ALARMING POPULATION GROWTH 35
1.6 TYPICAL INDIAN PSYCHE 42
Definition of a Superior Product 43
Big is Better 43
Money Talks and Walks 44
Gold Glitters 45
Branded & Designer 45
Donation & Bribery 46
Tall Poppy—We are the Best 46
Authority & Hierarchy 47
The Mainu Ki Attitude 48
Snobbish is Cool 49
Gender Bias 49
A Middle Life 57
General Characteristics 58
1.7 HAPPINESS & MONEY 59
1.7.1 Is India becoming happier? 59
1.7.2 Can Her Military Strength Make Her People Happy? 60
1.7.3 Does Love For Money Make People Happy? 60
1.7.4 Does Spending Money On Others Make People Happy? 62
Chapter 2 Summer 2016 - Welcome to India 64
2.0 AN UNSOLICITED ADVICE 64

2.1 A MEMORABLE AND UNUSUAL BREAKFAST ... 66
2.2 NATIONALISM – REALLY? ... 69
Chapter 3 Autumn 2016 – A Newfound Nationalism ... 76
3.0 WELCOME TO MUMBAI ... 76
3.1 TRAFFIC JAMS AND ROAD HAZARDS ... 80
3.2 ONE TO ONE PERSONAL INTERACTIONS ... 82
3.2.1 Symbolic Vegetarianism ... 83
3.2.2 Hollow Nationalism ... 86
3.2.3 Positive Conversations ... 87
3.3 AN AUSTRALIAN EXAMPLE OF NATIONALISM ... 100
Chapter 4 Winter of 2016 – Demonetisation ... 102
4.0 TRUE NATIONALISM ... 102
4.1 SHALLOW SOCIAL RELATIONS ... 105
4.2 MY WILL ... 106
4.3 BRAVE & GUTSY ENGINEERS ... 107
4.4 MINDLESS WEDDINGS ... 109
The traditions ... 109
Menu ... 110
Rituals ... 110
Noise ... 112
Chaos ... 112
Food ... 113
Wedding Cost ... 115
4.5 AN ALTERNATIVE MODEL ... 120
Chapter 5 Spring 2017 – An Unusual Dream Sequence ... 123
5.0 WELCOME TO DELHI ... 123

5.1 A BEAUTIFUL DREAM 124
5.2 A NIGHTMARE 129
Chapter 6 Going Forward 133
6.0 RECOGNISE THERE ARE ISSUES 133
6.1 WHAT DOES LIVING A LIFE MEAN? 134
6.1.1 Liveability & Peace 136
6.1.2 Health of a Country 138
6.2 AN ENGINEER'S APPROACH 141

CHAPTER 1
White-anting Issues

1.0 INTRODUCTION

About eight years ago, the specialist doctor said softly, yet with firmness and confidence in his voice, "She has Stage 4 cancer. It has spread out quite a bit in her body and it has also metastasised into her spine. As she is too weak to withstand any chemotherapy, there is not much that we can do." He did not use any sweetener; perhaps there was no need to use one in such a situation. He must have been trained at medical school to tackle such situations effectively with such calmness—a quick sharp cut to minimise the pain and the bleeding!

I did not faint or cry, as this was not the place and time to be emotional and weak. I had to be pragmatic and, therefore, needed to quickly digest the diagnosis. Without a quiver in my voice, I asked him after a deathly pause of a few seconds, "How long?" He replied quickly, with a distinct firmness in his voice, "A maximum of six months!"

My second and the last query was, "Is there anything that we can do for her?" This time, he replied slowly, with a hint of empathy in his voice, "Keep her as comfortable as you possibly can. Take her home. You may try radiotherapy if you want to lessen the pain."

The doctor's meeting was quick; it lasted for just about 15 minutes, so it seemed. That woman was my mother. Post that final advice from the doctor, my father and I looked into each other's eyes and decided to keep the news between us only. My mother never heard about her terminal condition till she died peacefully exactly a month later. She did not last for six months, as the doctor and we had hoped for.

What I am going to write in this book is about my other mother—my motherland—India. I am not an Indologist or anything; I am her son. So, given that we still have the time, if we can save her, let us do it.

This book is about the survival of future generations in India, to whom the current generation owes a moral, ethical and spiritual responsibility in looking after the sustainability of the country. This book is based on my common observations about daily life in parts of India that I frequently visit.

As one of my friends said, after his recent trip to India, "Things look generally okay in India, but mostly above the eye level; however, when you take a look at the ground, it is a bit scary."

Similar to the manner in which that doctor gave me that grave message, this book is intended to deliver a quick, sharp, and simple message, which even a middle school student should be able to understand. I don't want to limit the readership of this book to only the grown-ups, intellectuals and pseudo-intellectuals, many of whom will possibly judge this book and its author, based on the simplicity of its language or the author's political naivety.

I am conscious of the fact that, conceptually, simple is not considered to be cool in India; Indians like complexity—whether it is in written and spoken language, mundane issues, religion and spirituality, or designs of their clothes, houses or the main gate to their house.

In engineering design practice, it is the KISS[1] rule that is generally followed for sustainability and longevity of a structure or a product, and for ease of its manufacture /construction and maintenance. But most Indians seem too oblivious of this golden rule. Complex is cool for them.

---

[1] Acronym for 'Keep it Simple and Stupid'.

Albert Einstein once said, "*You do not really understand something unless you can explain it to your grandmother.*" Very often, each one of us comes across people who try to avoid answering simple questions, saying, "Ah! It is a bit complicated, you can't understand it." Sometimes, if you insist, such people may also just waffle around in answering very basic questions. In both such cases, one can only conclude that the other person has nothing but a raw and half-baked understanding of the subject matter.

A 19th Century visionary, social reformer and Chancellor of Iran, Amir Kabir[2], said:

- "*If you plan for a year, then grow wheat. If you plan for ten years, then grow trees, but if you plan for 100 years, then educate people.*"
- "*When I was young, I believed a good country needs a wise king. In my middle years, I believed a good country needs a wise vazir (Prime Minister). But now I know a good country needs wise and educated people.*"

Amir said the second quote a few months before his exile, following which he is believed to have been murdered by the establishment. It is always the people who make or break a nation; a government or a great leader can only do so much. A country is as good as its people. Unless the people are sincere and work responsibly for the good of their fellow citizens and, therefore, their country, no force in the world can change the destiny and fortune of a nation.

Let us now come back to the case that I am trying to make.

- "What comprises a country?" A simple answer would be: "a land mass, with human and other natural resources thriving on it."
- "How does a country survive?" A simple answer would be: "when her borders are protected, her citizens are physically

---

2 Amir Kabir (1807–10 January 1852), or Mirza Taghi Khan Farahani, is also known by titles of Atabak and Amir-e Nezam. He was the *Vazir* (Prime Minister) to Naser al-Din Shah Qajar (Shah of Persia). He is widely considered as Iran's first social reformer and one of the most capable, innovative and visionary persons of his time. Amir Kabir is believed to have been unjustly removed from his position, then exiled and finally murdered, as he gradually tried to reform Iran.

and mentally healthy, and she has abundant and sustainable natural resources."

All other things being equal, and keeping natural calamities and disasters out of the equation, a country will survive and progress only if her citizens are healthy and strong enough to look after not only themselves, but also their country's borders, environment and ecology; be able to effectively manage the country's natural resources; live a sustainable lifestyle; and leave their country in a better condition than what they had inherited.

1.1 WHY THIS BOOK?

I have been living outside India for more than 22 years but my roots are very much entrenched in India. Although I catch up with my father over the phone on a daily basis and my friends on a regular basis through popular social media, I visit India a number of times every year to catch up with my father, who lives at Jammu, and a number of my friends and relatives at Mumbai, Delhi and Srinagar (Kashmir).

"What is my problem then?" you may ask.

All overseas citizens and the NRIs who visit their home country on a regular basis understand the many challenges especially on the roads in India, during those short visits. For Indians living in India, it is just a way of life. Many may not even be aware of any better alternatives. They may not have many options but to simply accept the life as they see it and keep pressing on. In the course of fighting their life battles, sadly, many of them may not possibly know what lies ahead after just a few years!

"What is that common experience that you are talking about?" you may ask now. The answer is provided below.

I eagerly look forward to visiting India every now and then, albeit only on the good occasions. There have been unhappy times too in the past when I have had to make urgent trips to India, at very short notice, for example, to attend to my sick mother and then her funeral a number of years ago, followed by the funeral of my spiritual master a few years later and then my maternal uncle. At such times, when one fights one's internal demons, one should not have to fight the external demons too. During those distressful and unhappy times, covering 12,000 km each way is itself an ordeal and a huge challenge for one, both physically and mentally. Unfortunately, the distress that I have experienced during those hard times has been exacerbated by increasingly difficult living conditions in India. I recall one such occasion when I had just landed at Jammu Airport. I was on my way home to see my ailing mother when my taxi met with an accident on a very busy road, for no fault of my driver. The other driver was speaking to someone on his mobile phone at the time of the accident. He was rough and loud, seemingly wealthy and bullish, and managed to attract a large crowd. He physically beat my driver and openly stole some money from my driver's wallet. I looked on helplessly from my passenger seat.

Interestingly, each time, after a few days of my stay in India, I eagerly look forward to returning to my home in Australia. Every time, without fail, on my return to Australia, after travelling for nearly 13 hours (or sometimes more), when I step outside the air conditioned Perth International Airport terminal building, I immediately take a deep breath of fresh air and look up towards a deep blue sky. A refreshing thought flashes quickly through my mind, "I am finally home, thank God, I can breathe now." Thereafter, I quickly walk to the designated taxi stand and greet the driver of a waiting taxi in the queue. Out of respect for the taxi driver, and to uphold the inherent human dignity and the dignity of labour, as most other fellow Australians do, I invariably sit in the front of the taxi, to the left of the driver. Well, there are those new (London Cab) design taxis in the town, which do not allow the passenger to sit in the front of the taxi, for security reasons, mainly the driver's security[3].

3 There have been some unfortunate incidents in Australia involving Indian taxi drivers. When these drivers saw that their female passenger was drunk and/or wore a short skirt, they assumed the passenger was available for sex and then sexually assaulted her. That is exactly what many of their counterparts do in India. Little do these people know that wearing short skirts and being drunk is not a ticket for sex; it is nothing but a way of life of the passenger and her culture. Many Indians may outwardly look western but they continue to carry their orthodox Indian mentality and a sickening mindset, about the male dominance over females, wherever they go, only to find themselves behind bars after some time.

After fastening my seat belt, I invariably roll down the window, unless it is very hot outside, to allow the fresh air to come in and then constantly chat with my driver for the next half an hour till I reach home. It is just like a happy catch-up chat with a friend, generally about the weather, politics and sports.

Coming back to India, it would be reasonable to consider my experiences and observations, and those of millions of other tourists, as a barometer of the country's health.

With each visit to India, I find living conditions becoming increasingly difficult in the country, with more people, traffic, noise, smoke, dust etc. It makes me wonder, and extremely concerned, as to how the people will manage to live in the next 20 to 30 years, especially the children, when at present it so hard to:

- Find unpolluted air to breathe;
- Avoid contracting a range of debilitating mosquito borne diseases, such as malaria, dengue fever and chikungunya;
- Trust the quality of drinking water, both the tap water as well the commercially sold bottled water;
- Trust the quality of common alcoholic or non-alcoholic beverages being sold in India, including milk;
- Trust the quality of vegetables and fruits;
- Travel on the roads;
- Walk in the lanes and streets;
- Avoid serious airborne or waterborne diseases, such as typhoid and Hepatitis B;
- Avoid falling sick after eating commercially available food outside home; and
- Avoid dozes of antibiotics[4] during a short stay in India or immediately after returning from India.

---

[4] Some of these antibiotics, such as Azithral 500 (i.e. azithromycin), which are sold openly over the counter in India, cannot be prescribed by a doctor in Australia without receiving a written permission from the Australian Medical Council, a government body. In Australia, antibiotics cannot be bought over the counter; a valid registered doctor's prescription is required.

When I talk about India, I talk about India as a whole and not only her overly populated cities. About 70% of Indians live in villages; most are poor[5].

I recall in the seventies, when I was a young school going student, the sky used to look so blue and most people drank tap water. It was so easy to walk through the streets and move on the roads. Kids used to have plenty of playing areas around their house where they would play tennis-ball cricket, marbles or *gilli-danda,* or fly kites, depending upon the season of the year. All those things now seem to be a beautiful memory from a distant world of the past. Now the sky looks pale bluish grey; streets and roads are full of pedestrians and vehicles; and kids have lost their playing areas to residential and commercial structures. In these past 40 years, the country has become more populated, technologically advanced, militarily stronger, but she has not progressed at all in terms of the basic requirements of life—air, water, food etc. The quality of all these basic essentials of life has nosedived. People are indeed living longer, perhaps due to advances in medical science and medication; but can that be called living a life when most Indians, on an average, need to consume a course of antibiotics every month? I recall a famous dialogue spoken in a 70's movie (*Mr Natwarlal*) by Indian iconic actor, Amitabh Bachchan, "*Arre yeh jeena bhi koi jeena hai, Lallu*?" ("Can this life be called living a life, my dear?")

You may ask, "What is life other than what millions of Indians are living at the present?" In my view and in the view of millions of people like me worldwide, life does not mean just existence, consumption and procreation. For humans to claim to be different from other animals, such as chimpanzees and gorillas, living life is much beyond all these activities. There are over 7.4 billion people living on the planet as we speak and no two human beings are alike or think alike. The answer to the question "what defines life?" depends on who is asking. Each one of us sees this world differently, depending on our end conditions, and tries to make some sense out of it.

---

5 *The Seattle Times,* dated 3 July 2015, with reference to India's socio economic and caste census data collected between 2011 and 2013.

The definition of life is very individual specific. For a poor person in India, life may mean to be able to survive, make both ends meet and, with time, become rich and possess all known comforts of the world—a house, a car, electronic gadgets, expensive clothes, rich food and plenty of cash.

For a rich person, however, life may mean becoming richer and owning everything out there—properties and assets, land, people and become God, if possible.

For a spiritual person, though, life may mean pursuit of the truth and promoting oneness, peace and harmony amongst various life forms on the planet. For a philosopher, life may mean to contemplate and try to decipher what it is all about. In the words of Thoreau[6]:

"*Most of the luxuries and many of the so-called comforts of life are not only not indispensable, but positive hindrances to the elevation of mankind.*"

Is life, therefore, an opportunity for us for our inner (spiritual) elevation? Following his two year long experiment at Walden Pond, about living a simple life in the woods, Thoreau penned the following words in his book *Walden*:

"*I went to the woods because I wished to live deliberately, to front only the essential facts of life, and see if I could not learn what it had to teach, and not, when I came to die, discover that I had not lived. I did not wish to live what was not life, living is so dear; nor did I wish to practise resignation, unless it was quite necessary. I wanted to live deep and suck out all the marrow of life, to live so sturdily and Spartan-like as to put to rout all that was not life, to cut a broad swath and shave close, to drive life into a corner, and reduce it to its lowest terms, and, if it proved to be mean, why then to get the whole and genuine meanness of it, and publish its meanness to the world; or if it were sublime,*

---

6 Ref. Wikipedia. Henry David Thoreau (12 July 1817–6 May 1862) was an American philosopher of nature, an essayist, poet, abolitionist, naturalist, surveyor and historian. For nearly two years, between 4 July 1845 and 6 September 1847, he lived in a small hut, which he built himself on the shores of Walden Pond in Boston (US), about 2.4 km from his family home.

to know it by experience, and be able to give a true account of it in my next excursion."

This book aims to raise a general awareness amongst the Indian masses about the issues that, in my eyes, are white-anting[7] the general life in India, and the country in the process, despite many Indian citizens tirelessly working to address these issues or making some noise about them. Unfortunately, such acts of active citizenship end up being unseen or falling upon deaf ears of powerful people who have the potential to make things happen but choose not to do anything and millions who just don't care. A majority of the Indians, caught up with their daily struggles to live and make both ends meet, are either completely oblivious of the issues, or too ignorant or even too lazy to bother about them. How unfortunate it is that many people in this country, particularly those in power and with resources, choose to turn a blind eye to a number of such issues, which look straight into their eyes as soon as they leave their home and travel on the road.

If there are people, with consciousness and morality, who are aware and alive to some of these issues, logically they should be able to do something to control and eradicate them. But, if the people themselves become white-ants, there is not much that one can do. The way the Indian population has been growing over past seven decades, it won't be an unreasonable hypothesis that the people themselves seem to be white-anting the country.

In the next 20 years, the quality of air, water and food should logically dive further down, unless something is done now on a war footing. In another 20 years or so, people will definitely find it increasingly hard to breathe the natural air. Many may not be able to breathe at all without the use of portable oxygen cylinders. Many families have already installed air purifiers in their bedrooms in Delhi.

---

[7] White ants are also called termites. White-anting is an Australian term for the process of internal erosion of a foundation. It is often used in reference to groups such as political parties or organisations where information from group insiders is 'leaked' or used to undermine the goals of the group (Ref. https://en.wikipedia.org/wiki/White-anting)

But what do they do once they have to move outside? One can't always be holed up in an air-conditioned bedroom and breathe the purified air? The whole country needs a gigantic air-purifier.

The local sources of drinking water will dwindle and become more unfit for human consumption. The groundwater for irrigation purposes and, therefore, the local agricultural produce will become more toxic and potentially unfit for human and animal consumption. The rich and affluent class may, however, be able to survive on imported bottled water and canned food. Life will find it extremely hard to be able to move through the arteries of the country (streets and roads). Perhaps, only the rich may be able to move, that too by flying around with the help of drones. Possibly, most of the rich may also have completely deserted the country.

Most of India's problems can reasonably and logically be attributed to (a) her ever-growing and seemingly unmanageable population across the country; and (b) a continuous migration of people from rural to urban parts of India. That is why so much polluted air and adulterated milk, adulterated food and spurious medicines are being fed to the children in that country. Wise people may dismiss this, saying, "If we are able to reduce the rate of population growth, it should not matter." I would argue that the natural resources will keep dwindling with time and not keep increasing. With time, it will become increasingly difficult to feed people, as the paddy and agriculture land is fast being converted into residential and commercial development, and farmers are committing suicide every year for various reasons, including climate change, global warming and drought. Therefore, who will grow the food, how and where? If the country is struggling now to provide pure air, water and food to the existing population, how can one imagine she will be able to support any future growth? India does not have endless and inexhaustible natural resources; no country has. There is a limit to everything, i.e. at the maximum, how many people can be fed and with how much quantity?

Interestingly, while obesity is on the rise in India in relatively more affluent class due to greed and over-consumption of food, millions are underweight due to malnourishment. A dumbbell shaped social structure, such as the one we are witnessing now, will potentially collapse one day; it is not sustainable.

It would be useful if the current Indian youth and their leaders in Indian universities, such as Kanhaya and Hardik Patel, and the student bodies like ABVP and NSUI, channelize their focus and energy in starting a nationwide campaign and educate people about these pressing issues (and their looming repercussions) for saving their country not only for the sake of their own children but also for all future generations yet to arrive in India. Otherwise, as the nation seems to bask under the glory of the recent progresses made by it in numerous fields, it may potentially choke itself to a standstill in a couple of decades from now.

While most people in India are working hard to make both ends meet, and some people hardly working, a number of ground issues are silently white-anting the country. One can imagine how silently and clandestinely termites eat the timber. It is extremely heartbreaking to see that rich people in India are busy becoming richer and politically powerful; the middle class are striving hard to climb the social ladder and move close to the upper class; the politicians are playing politics, which is becoming dirtier with time, and continuously throwing mud on one another; bureaucrats are busy keeping people happy and constantly trying to stay in control of the real power; and an average Indian is too busy and fatigued to do anything meaningful. Perhaps, he has given up on humans and is now waiting for Nature to set things right! Well, that wish and expectation is not unreasonable; Nature always has the last laugh when man fiddles too much with Her!

Can God help, considering India is a very religious country? Isn't there a mushrooming growth of places of worship in India? And don't people offer big chunks of gold, diamonds and money, as bribe, to their Gods? Don't people fight one another based on their religious faiths? Isn't religion a bigger deal in India than the survival of the country itself? Maybe only God can help to save the country and, hopefully, I'll then be able to visit her even after 20 years. Hopefully!

For God's sake, let us think deeply, provided we are still able to think, considering the cumulative effect of heavy metals which may have possibly already made inroads into our brains through a continued consumption of polluted air, contaminated water and contaminated food over the last few decades.

It is nice to keep one's head above the clouds and only enjoy what is pristine, glorious and the infinite, but it is equally important to make sure the ground which supports our feet is also strong enough for eternity and not be consumed by the white-ants, as it seems to be happening now. It is only a matter of time before the whole structure collapses due to its weakened foundations as a result of an uncontrolled termite activity.

History is continuously being written. Civilisations have come and gone. Prophets too have come and gone. The world keeps moving—nothing in this world is stationary. India's collective destiny will take her where she is destined to go. If people wake up and help themselves, things can change, given that they still have time on their side—not everything is lost, not yet, as we speak. As they say, "*a stitch in time saves nine.*" It is also said, "*God helps those who help themselves.*" As for the urgency, they say, "*Time and tide wait for none.*" As for me, I don't want to die with regret that I did not do anything to save my motherland, not even made a little noise.

I am sure that I am not the first one to raise these issues, nor will be the last one to do so. All I am doing is to add my little voice to a growing chorus across India, and possibly across the world, that is urging and begging all Indians to do something to address these issues. The first thing that I am asking is to stop any further increase in the population for at least next five to ten years. Mother India has already too many people to feed; she will not be in a position to feed anyone in a few decades from now if demands from her increasing population keep increasing, even at a relatively slower rate; every new arrival will increase the demand on the existing resources, which will potentially keep thinning out with time. It is understood that the rate of population may have slowed down a shade, but that is not good enough. If we are already too many, we can't afford more. Just let the birth-rate match the death rate, or preferably be lower than death rate, and don't allow the population to increase any further in the next decade or so, while the government will keep working hard to address other national issues.

Let us follow the Indian Prime Minister, Mr Modi. He is a fine example of offering personal sacrifice for the sake of serving one's country. He does not have any biological children of his own; he has long adopted the whole country as his family. Just follow his example and adopt the country; look after those children who are born in lower socio-economic communities and those who struggle to live. Who else in the country works harder than him? Who else in the country sleeps just four hours every night and works tirelessly in the remaining hours—thinking, worrying, travelling, and doing things?

Sadly, why do we bring more people into this world if we can't give them a happy and healthy life? Don't we have a moral responsibility towards our children and all future generations, or do we behave just like a swarm of locusts that devours everything in its way and then dies? What is the need to produce your own child when so many children in India need shelter and help to survive? Just adopt them. If Australians can do it, why can't Indians do it for their own people?

A recent Australian film, titled *Lion*, is about one such child (named *Saru*–distorted from *Sheru*) who luckily found a home in Australia after he went missing from his home in India about three decades ago, when he was around 5 years old. As destiny would have it, he was extremely fortunate to have been adopted by a young Australian couple, who chose not have any children of their own after they adopted him and another Indian child.

1.1.1 What Comprises a Healthy Living?

Let us now try to answer the core question: what does it take humans to survive and be healthy? In addition to having peace of mind, which is so vital in these fast, competitive and relatively corrosive times, a logical answer would be the availability of:

- Free clean air to breathe
- Free potable water to drink
- Unadulterated and fresh food to eat
- Genuine medicines when one becomes sick

- Appropriate seasonal clothing to wear
- A comfortable shelter called home
- Safety and security at home and outside home
- Enough physical and mental activity to remain physically and mentally alert and healthy
- Harmony amongst people for a healthy social life
- Good spiritual health for internal happiness

If the above basics are not freely available to our current generations, how can one expect the country will survive for long, given that her future generations will find it extremely hard to stay healthy and be able to survive? They will have to potentially pay for the sins—consumerism, short-sightedness, negligence and ignorance of the current generations in India.

Alarmingly, the country does not even figure amongst the happiest countries in the world, despite best efforts of Bollywood, numerous television channels, spiritual preachers and yoga gurus. The country seems to be paying a high price for capitalism, corruption, and population (CCP).

If the country is not very happy, and the living conditions are not very healthy, what are we actually achieving through material progress? Shouldn't good health, contentment and peace be the main objectives of life? What does prosperity mean without happiness and peace of mind?

1.2 INDIA'S OUTSTANDING ACHIEVEMENTS

Indians must deservedly be proud of numerous achievements that the country has made in the last 70 years after independence in almost all walks of life—science and technology, sports, economy and eradication of some diseases. The following is a list of some, if not all, of these achievements.

- The third largest economy in the world;
- Fastest growing economy in the world, with GDP rate of more than 7%;
- Home to 101 billionaires, i.e. the world's fourth highest number of billionaires, as per *The Times of India*, dated 21 March 2017;

- Second largest producer of food, after China;
- Home to one of the best IT industries in the world;
- Attracts medical tourism through her first class medical services at relatively much cheaper costs;
- An advanced space programme—Mangalyaan to Mars; successful launching of satellites in space for foreign countries, including the recent launch of record 104 satellites in a single attempt; and the perceived capability to develop and create an indigenous space station;
- Indigenous missile technology;
    - Ballistic missiles, such as SRBM—the Prithvi range; IRBM—the Agni range I to IV; and ICBM—Agni V and VI.
    - Cruise missiles (e.g. Brahmos and Nirbhay).
    - Surface to air missiles, such as Trishul, Akash and Nag.
    - Ship defence surface to air missiles, such as K Series missiles and Barak Series missiles.
- A member of eight sovereign countries that have successfully detonated nuclear weapons and have a large nuclear weapons arsenal;
- World's largest English speaking youth power—with largest youth population (10-24 year olds) and approximately 65% of population below the age of 35 years;
- World's largest English speaking population and the 2nd largest population (after the US) of *fluent* English speakers (150 to 250 million);
- One of the largest workforce of professionals—engineers, doctors and other key professionals;
- More than 35 million, economically successful, non-resident Indians living across the planet;
- Third largest army in the world after China and the US, with the second largest paramilitary force in the world;
- Fourth largest air force in the world, with a recent induction of its second indigenously manufactured combat aircraft. India is also developing the fifth generation stealth aircraft;

- Fifth largest navy in the world, with sophisticated missile-capable warships, two aircraft carriers, minesweepers, advanced submarines, with a significant use of state of the art technology that is indigenously manufactured; plans to induct the INS Vikrant by 2018 followed by a larger INS Vishal.

In addition:

- India is one of two ancient civilizations (other one being Chinese), dating back to at least 5000 years, which have stood the test of time and survived against all odds.
- Indians are believed to have invented the numbering system (introduced into the West by Arabic mathematicians, Arabic numerals), the concept of zero, logic, geometry, basic algebra, calculus, probability, astronomy etc.
- The Indian cultural influence has historically spread, through the philosophy of religions like Buddhism, Hinduism, Sikhism, etc., to foreign lands through traders, philosophers and migration. According to the Chinese ambassador to the United States, Hu Shih, "India conquered and dominated China culturally for 20 centuries without ever having to send a single soldier across her border."
- The Indian film industry, being the largest in the world, has played a major role in spreading the Indian culture worldwide. Indian films are popular in central and west Asia, south-east Asia, Africa, and are now becoming increasingly popular in the Western society—the US, the UK, Australia, New-Zealand, and Canada.
- The Indian cricket team is one of the top cricket teams in the world. Currently, in test cricket, India ranks No 1 in the world.
- In many other sports, such as badminton, tennis, wrestling, boxing, shooting and golf, many Indian players have started making a mark for themselves by not only winning tournaments but also Olympic and world championship medals.

- In addition to the above, Indians are living longer[8] than before and becoming more affluent with time.

On a sad note, the Indian growth and prosperity is accompanied by an alarming increase in the rate of mental illnesses[9], including depression, and suicide. As per the world reports, India is not one of world's happiest or healthiest countries.

Many young Indians are extremely intelligent people. However, in their pursuit of knowing everything, they lose the core objective of living the life itself. Alarmingly, many have fallen in love with artificial intelligence and live in a virtual world. Thanks to the internet and

---

8 *The Times of India*, dated 29 January 2014, presented the statistics released by the Union Ministry of Health & Family Welfare, which indicated that life expectancy in India had increased by about five years for males from 62.3 years in 2001-2005 to 67.3 years in 2011-2015; and for females from 63.9 years in 2001-2005 to 69.6 years in 2011-2015. This rate of increase was found to be higher than that in the previous decade. The reasons were identified as better immunization and nutrition, coupled with prevention and treatment of infectious diseases. In comparison, the World Health Organisation (WHO) 2015 data indicated that in the developed world, people lived around 15 to 20 years longer than the Indians. Of the 183 countries, India ranked 125 in terms of life expectancy for both genders.
In India, the average life expectancy was around 42 years in 1960. It steadily climbed to around 48 in 1980, 58.5 years in 1990 and around 62 years in 2000.

9 The online version of Indian newspaper, *Hindustan Times,* dated 27 Feb 2017, in its editorial published an article, titled *Depression on the rise but India does not have a policy for the mentally ill.* As per the article, in 2015, WHO estimated five crore Indians suffering from depression and over three crores from anxiety disorders. Depression is a major cause of mental disability worldwide, with more women affected by depression than men. At its worst, depression can lead to suicide.
The editorial added, that in India, this disease has always been brushed under the carpet and, therefore, the condition festers unheeded till it spirals out of control.
Mental illness is defined as "a substantial disorder of thinking, mood, perception, orientation or memory that grossly impairs judgment, behaviour, capacity to recognise reality or ability to meet the ordinary demands of life, mental conditions associated with the abuse of alcohol and drugs, but does not include mental retardation, which is a condition of arrested or incomplete development of mind of a person, specially characterised by sub-normality of intelligence."

the social media, the actual face-to-face inter-human interaction is dwindling at a considerable rate.

The educated young and older people alike widely use social media but, unfortunately, their topics are limited to local, national and world politics, albeit some extremely petty and meaningless, and videos on PM Modi, Mr Rahul Gandhi and President Trump; and jokes on wives and husbands.

It is sad to see that an overwhelming majority of the Indian population is oblivious to more serious national and social issues.

1.3 A DISTINCT INDIAN EXPERIENCE

This section outlines my experiences and observations during my visits to India, as well as the media reports, and summarises what actually is on the ground, i.e. what India should be and what India actually is!

1.3.1 A Familiar and Distinct Indian Odour

As soon as one steps out of the plane, and starts walking through a waiting vestibule, a strong but familiar and quintessentially Indian odour in the air greets the visitor—which appears to be born out of a relatively damp indoor environment, air-conditioned air and the overall polluted air quality outdoors.

The smell clings to everything—a person's body, clothes, even the washed and ironed clothes that one packs in the bag at the time of departure from India. It accompanies one all the way to ones overseas destination and does not leave till the clothes are washed. This characteristic Indian smell lurks in ones nostrils till one is in India and then sticks to ones brain forever.

A ten-year-old Indian kid commented immediately after being hugged by his maternal grandfather, who had just arrived from India, "Nanu[10], you smell so Indian." No one in the room could understand at that time what he meant. So, his mother asked him, 'Does your Dadu[11] (also an Indian but living in Melbourne) also smell Indian?",

10 Maternal grandfather

11 Paternal grandfather

and he said "no". It did not take very long for everyone around to decipher what he meant.

1.3.2 Immigration

Immigration counters practically mark the border of the host country. It is not unusual to see some overworked, stern looking immigration staff receiving visitors without any smile or any expression on their faces. Understandably, their job is to make sure that they allow only the genuine visitors, with valid visa etc., to enter the country. In simple words, they want to make sure that you are the person that you claim to be. I have no problem with any of that. After having lived in Australia for nearly two decades, and having travelled widely across the globe, all that I would like to see is a customary smile on the face of the immigration officer, as a welcome gesture. After all, he is the first representative of the host country. A warm smile will indeed go a long way in having a positive psychological effect on the mind of the visitor and make him feel welcome. They say the first impression is the last impression. Humans must respect the inherent dignity of other humans. A host must respect the guest—that is universal.

Atithi Devo Bhava, which means the guest is equivalent to God, is the official slogan of the country and her tourism department. It would be encouraging to see the immigration staff invoking this ancient Hindu code of conduct for hospitality.

India is a great tourist destination and tourists bring in a lot of money to the country, which helps a range of local businesses. A tourist is also a means of spreading a good image of the host country. And a country means her people. Therefore, the behaviour and personal conduct of people in India, including government officials and businessmen, plays an important role in terms of hospitality. The Indian culture proudly claims to practice the concept of *Atithi Devo Bhava*, but the general mindset is interwoven with a hypocritical approach, which is sad, as a result of which the cultural concept (of treating guests like god) becomes vague and invalid.

Mere campaigning of *Atithi Devo Bhava* is not enough; it must be a part of the general Indian mindset and practice, and not just a cultural concept.

1.3.3 Checked-in Baggage

Usually, it can take a bit of time to receive your checked-in baggage. Normally, I choose to stand near the inlet of the belt to be able to identify my bag as soon as it is appears on the conveyor.

There is always a risk of losing sight of your baggage, as it may be offloaded by a baggage worker from the belt after making its first round, near the exiting window, in order to create more space on the belt. In December 2016, I met a fellow traveller who kept on waiting for his baggage for more than an hour. After all other passengers had received their bags and vacated the area, he found his bags had been offloaded by a worker during its first round only and kept to one side.

In addition, one can't rule out the possibility that a fellow passenger can take away your bag, inadvertently by mistake or deliberately on purpose. In India, unlike airports in Australia, thorough custom checks are rarely observed, so it is very easy for anyone to carry away someone else's bag. In Australia, most bags undergo X-ray screening and physical checks after the passenger is asked to stand in a custom clearance queue. No one can leave the airport without a thorough check by the custom officials.

1.3.4 Polluted Air

My immediate fears and common observations, as soon as I leave the airport terminal building, are summarised in the following bullet points:

- Potential risk to develop a cough, especially during monsoons and the winter months, as the quality of air always seems to have deteriorated since the last time, with more dust and smoke particles suspended in the air, which can carry a disease; although this also depends on the weather and the season at the time of my arrival. One must quickly adjust to the air quality in order to breathe and there is no escape. Experience has it that, in many cases, the cough contracted in India can take up to two months or so to go away, particularly if sinuses are infected. In addition, a regular intake of bad polluted air can lead to lung, brain diseases and premature deaths[12].

The online version of *The Times of India*, dated 4 March 2017, published an article[13], titled "*Pollution is causing life-giving rain to become increasingly acidic in many parts of the country*", based on a research by Indian Meteorological Department and Indian Institute of Tropical Meteorology. So, one does not really know what kind of air and aerosols one is actually breathing in. You could be breathing anything!

- There is a risk of getting bitten by mosquitoes and contracting potential diseases like malaria, dengue and chikungunya, especially during the humid autumn months. Of these,

---

12 The online version of *Times of India*, dated 15 February 2017, reported that India tops the list of countries in ozone pollution deaths, as per the State of Global Air report, released in Boston, MA (USA). India accounts for the highest number of premature deaths due to ozone pollution, 13 times more than Bangladesh and 21 times more than Pakistan.

On 19 February 2017, the online version of *The Times of India*, based on a prestigious medical journal, *The Lancet*, reported that two Indians die every minute in India (i.e. over a million Indians die every year) due to air pollution. The report also said that some of the world's most polluted cities are in India, which include Delhi and Patna.

13 The results of analysis of rainwater samples collected from various parts of India between 2001-2012 have showed a pH level of 4.77 to 5.32, which is less than 7 and therefore, indicates 'acid rain'. Its formation is possibly a result of atmospheric moisture / water getting mixed with gaseous emissions, such as oxides of sulphur and nitrogen, from vehicles, industries and thermal power plants.

Acid rain has the potential to kill the aquatic life and also affect the growth and productivity of plants and crops due to leaching of soil nutrients from the soil. Acid rain also corrodes structures. On a much more serious and alarming note, acid rain dissolves heavy metal salts in rocks and soil and carries them to agriculture fields and into the groundwater, which finally reaches the human body.

As per scientists, V Vizaya Bhaskar and P S P Rao (Ref Journal of Atmospheric Chemistry), almost all global atmosphere watch (GAW) stations in India have shown a decreasing trend in pH levels with each passing decade between 1981 and 2012, which must be alarming to all Indians.

dengue and chikungunya are extremely debilitating and can potentially be fatal in many cases. For this reason, I wear a full sleeved shirt and long trousers during my journey. But, is that foolproof? No. The risk always exists.

1.3.5 Transport & Traffic

Every visitor looks for a safe and comfortable mode of transportation to reach his destination in India. The following are my general observations and experiences while moving outdoors in India, which start from the airport itself:

- The potential risk of engaging a wrong taxi from the airport—although this risk has reduced with time, as more regulations have been introduced by the government. Although by choosing popular taxi services, such as Meru, Ola, Uber etc., one can reduce the risk, but due to the possibility of a rogue taxi driver, the potential of getting robbed, raped or murdered always remains, especially during late night hours. So, till the moment I do not reach my destination, within a reasonable travel time and a reasonable taxi fare, I remain a bit nervous and vigilant, and make sure I don't doze off in the taxi due to travel and fatigue. Unlike most people in India, I sit on the front seat of the taxi, to the left of the driver (in line with my practice in Australia, for human dignity) and try to engage the driver in some interesting, but general conversation, such as related to current politics, social issues, family or sports.
- One can also engage an auto-rickshaw. But, in that case, the probability of the risk of catching an annoying chest infection or developing a niggling cough, especially during the winter months increases significantly.

  A couple of years ago, a 20 minute travel experience in an auto-rickshaw, engaged for its versatility of movement through relatively narrow lanes and very narrow by-lanes, to avoid a massive traffic jam on the main road, resulted in two dozes of antibiotics for both my wife and I. We had to continue medication upon our arrival in Perth for another two weeks. The reasons are that we don't have any immunity to the seasonal bugs in India. In addition, in Australia, we consume basic antibiotics, albeit strictly on doctor's prescription. However, due to an increasing drug resistance in India (due to careless misuse of antibiotics by people or due to spurious medication), one has to use the most updated antibiotic in India to combat the updated bug strain.

- More vehicles[14] seem to be running on the roads, with heavier traffic and relatively more congestion, and an increased travel time since my last visit. It is very frustrating at times and a pure waste of time when one has to allow three to four hours for travelling a distance of 20 to 30 km in India, for example to reach the nearest airport or a railway station. The frustration gets compounded when you are rushing to take your international flight and the road is unexpectedly blocked by the traffic police because a certain VIP (India has numerous VIPs) is supposed to cross an adjacent cross road. Furthermore, in India, I feel very giddy and nauseated even after travelling for 10 minutes as a passenger in a car. The travel sickness is exacerbated by the way people drive their cars, which includes frequent change of lanes followed by sudden braking and sudden acceleration. For me, being on the road is like living in hell and this experience keeps on getting worse with each trip.
- With each visit, more and more people seem to be walking on the roads and riding bicycles/motorcycles/ scooters through the existing streets and narrow lanes. This makes walking in the streets or crossing a road a chore and very risky for a pedestrian. Even in those narrow lanes and by-lanes, where one would not expect any fast moving motorcycle to move, one gets startled when you hear a vehicle coming from behind,

[14] The online version of *The Times of India*, dated 18 August 2016, reported 53,700 vehicles hitting the roads across the country every day. The paper quoted an Urban Transport expert, N Ranganathan, saying that India had around 18.6 crore (1 crore = 10 Millions) vehicles in August 2016, which would increase to 35 crores in the next 20 to 30 years. He also said that 7% growth in GDP would translate into a 10% growth in demand for transport.

which forces you to suddenly jump across the nearest side drain to save yourself or risk being hit or run over. On a rainy day, your clothes can be sprayed with mud and muddy water when such a two-wheeler runs through a puddle of water, which is a common sight.

- In India, most roads and streets look like malls, with mixed traffic—humans, animals, bicycles, motorcycles, and both light and heavy motorised vehicular traffic.
- Most traffic jams are man-made—due to ignorance of driving rules and poor education. How many people go to a registered driving school to learn driving and then pass a stringent driving test before getting their driver's license? Public transport and private vehicles are allowed to drop and pick passengers at the road intersections, which turn out to be the worst bottlenecks. It is common sense not to clog road intersections, but that *common sense* does not seem to be very common in India. In comparison, in Australia, no vehicle can stop within a distance of 50 metres or so from a road crossing.
- Has anyone counted the cost of traffic jams and longer driving time on the economy and health of the country—in terms of wasted time, higher fuel consumption, harmful emissions, driver fatigue and mental illness? If yes, has any meaningful and visible action been undertaken? Apparently not, the way I see it!

1.3.6 Drinking Water

The quality of drinking water cannot be trusted in India. The first thing that I ask my host is, "Can I drink this water? I don't have the immunity to consume normal tap water in India." Many people understand and assure me, "Yes, it is safe to drink; it is from our RO (Reverse Osmosis) system."

There are many homes that I visit who don't have an RO system. At such places, I prefer to take boiled tea. Some people offer bottled mineral water, but who does not know that a significantly large percentage of bottled mineral water is nothing but normal tap water.

My father at Jammu has adopted a double protection method—he boils the water that comes out of the RO system before it is consumed. For safety, he always carries from home a large (1.5 Litre) bottle of water with him whenever he steps outside him home, whether for shopping or socialising. He never consumes water that is sold commercially in India, as he doubts its authenticity and purity. As for fizzy, carbonated soft drinks, he trusts only the canned drinks, and not the bottled versions. He says canned drinks are factory sealed in Maharashtra, whereas bottled versions contain local groundwater, which may contain undesired chemicals, including heavy metals.

In Australia, most people consume the normal tap water, so such issues never arise.

In situations where water quality is seriously doubtful, it is prudent that one goes for hard boiled tea. I want to see a day when I can fearlessly trust the tap water in India.

1.3.7 Fruits, Vegetables& Dairy products

The definition of healthy food is pretty much universal in the world. It includes plenty of fruits and vegetables. In Australia, to combat a growing obesity trend, for the last decade or so, the government has been trying to promote healthy food (via 2 & 5 campaign) for good health through a daily intake of a minimum of two servings of fruits and five servings of vegetables. Eating plenty of fruits and vegetables is known to protect one against a number of diseases and helps to maintain a healthy weight. However, I am not very sure if all fruit sold in India by the vendors can be trusted as fit for human consumption. Even many resident Indians don't trust it and avoid feeding any fruit to their children, with of course some health consequences. As for vegetables, I can't afford to eat any salad or any uncooked vegetables.

Adulterated vegetables

In India, one can't eat salads and uncooked vegetables without risking one's health. Some vegetables can't be trusted even after being cooked. A few years ago, some serious health issues were reported in Delhi and neighbouring areas due to intake of cabbage. Perhaps the origin of the vegetable and the quality of water used for its cultivation could be blamed. As vegetables don't exhibit their origins and the source of water used for their growth, a deep element of distrust about their purity remains on the mind of a consumer. Vegetables and fruits that are grown in polluted and toxic areas, such as around the Yamuna River belt in Delhi and surrounding areas, are believed to be fed with river water that can potentially contain toxic chemicals and heavy metals.

Adulterated fruit

Similar to vegetables, fruits can also be contaminated or doctored. It is a common practice in the country that many fruits, such as watermelons, are injected with coloured sweetened water to look red and taste sweet. Well, that may not be such a big issue as long as permissible food colours are used and the injected coloured water is potable. I have historically suffered from diarrhoea and severe gastroenteritis caused by the consumption of tempered/spurious fruit in India. In the past, I have been very lucky to have travelled and reached Perth alive after I had sudden diarrhoea and started throwing up a few hours before commencing my return journey from Jammu.

Also, poisonous chemicals, like calcium carbide (CaC_2)[15], are used for fast (artificial) ripening of fruit, such as papayas, bananas, mangoes and citrus fruits. Calcium carbide is a known carcinogen, which means it can alter human cells into cancer cells. During my last trip to India,

---

[15] When calcium carbide comes in contact with moisture, it produces acetylene gas, which acts like ethylene, which is the natural ripening agent, and accelerates the ripening process. Industrial-grade calcium carbide use for ripening in India may also contain traces of arsenic and phosphorus, which are carcinogenic.
The online version of *Mail Today*, dated 28 June 2015, reported that, although calcium carbide is illegal for use as an artificial ripening agent in most countries, it is being freely used across India to artificially accelerate the ripening process of several fruits, such as mangoes, watermelons, bananas etc. just to scale up the sales.
"*Calcium carbide leads to skin allergies and rashes and at times can also cause a severe disease like skin cancer. Since most of the fruits procured from the market are artificially ripened, the only way to skim the carbide content is to wash the fruits properly. The use of this chemical should be stopped completely in order to wipe out the risk of cancerous diseases,*" a Delhi-based skin specialist, Dr AK Dadhwal, has said.

in December 2016, my father-in-law developed a severe skin allergy around his lips after consuming a (seemingly innocent) banana.

Now if you know all this, can you eat fruits and vegetables in India without risking your health? Imagine how it is going to be in future! We can just imagine the general condition of health of adults and children alike who don't consume the recommended quantities of fruits and vegetables due to common concerns about their authenticity and contamination. The country is seemingly producing a relatively sick generation who are missing out on healthy food.

Adulterated dairy, poultry & meat

As with fruits, we can't trust the authenticity and quality of milk and other dairy products.

Reportedly, there is a 68% probability (roughly two out of three chances) that the milk that you are consuming in India, in the form of milk, yoghurt, ice-cream, Indian sweets, kheer, cheese, tea or coffee, is adulterated[16] with caustic soda, detergents, glucose, white paint or refined oil.

Fortunately, I am a vegan vegetarian. I don't consume milk, yoghurt or cheese in India. Therefore, I don't need to be bothered about the quality and authenticity of milk or milk products or poultry or meat or fish wherever I live or go. But it is not all about me. It is about the millions of children living in India, who consume a range of dairy products and, of course, the adults, who consume a range of animal foods, let alone millions of unsuspecting foreign tourists who visit the country every year, whose health is seriously compromised through the food intake in India and that too without their knowledge.

Can you trust the assurances provided by your Indian host (family, relatives, friends, hotels, cafés', restaurants) about the quality of food being served to you? No, certainly not. No one can provide any guarantee to you that the food that is being served to you is not

---

[16] The Online version of *The Times of India*, dated 17 March 2016, reported that over 68% of the milk sold in India was found to be adulterated in a 2011 Food Safety and Standards Authority of India (FSSAI) study.

adulterated. Why? Just because they wouldn't know themselves if it is absolutely unadulterated, doctored or contaminated!

If I were a resident of India and playing a host, I would be very careful in making any assurance to my guest with regard to the quality of food that I would be serving. Using a quasi-legal but absolutely reasonable language, I would assure my guest, even swear, "*To the extent I know and can reasonably control its quality, the food being served to you is clean and safe to consume.*" With this assertion, I would be transferring the ball into the court of my guest. Therefore, it would be up to my guest to decide what to eat and what not to eat and how much to eat, at his/her own absolute risk.

As for fish, one can't be certain about their source. They could be sourced from waters, such as *nallahs* (stormwater and open drains) that are rich in heavy metals and arsenic, let alone other nasty stuff.

As for meat and poultry, I wouldn't like to write much for religious connotations and interpretations; it can be an extremely sensitive issue.

Personally, I don't believe in animal killing for food consumption. Humans should have a long time ago moved from the lives of our distant ancestors—cave dwellers, hunters and gatherers and adopted food habits dissimilar to other meat eating animals.

We have a Siberian husky as our pet at home. His dinner, which is his main meal, generally comprises raw chicken carcass and cooked lamb mince, with rice and carrots. Over time, even he has shown a strong preference for fruits (apples, watermelon, pears, bananas and mangoes) and cooked vegetables.

1.3.8 Spurious and Fake Medicines

Can you trust medicines in India? Maybe or maybe not! It depends upon how much you know about the mode of their manufacture but, more alarmingly, how much you don't know. My father at Jammu buys his medicines only from a few selected outlets, as he does not trust all medical stores. He thinks that he consumes *safe* medicines, but only God knows!

A few years ago, I watched a documentary in Australia about a sudden surge in the deaths at a hospital in Africa. A follow-up investigation by a dedicated investigative journalist revealed that the deaths had occurred due to spurious medicines. The investigator followed the trail of medicines and finally landed in India, which was found to be the source country. He interviewed many people in India. To our shock, we found that many so-called medicines were made in the backyards and basements of homes of many private citizens; many tablets and capsules comprised just chalk and many injectable medicines comprised just distilled water.

In the documentary, many people asked the interviewer, "Just tell us which strength of a particular drug (medicine) you want, and we'll give you. If you want a 100% pure and genuine medicine, we'll make it for you but you'll have to pay a high cost for it, and your profits will be less. If you want a medicine of 50% strength, you pay just half and make money. If you pay for 25% strength, you will pay less and make much more money. Tell us what you want and we will give you that."

The online version of *India Spend*, dated 15 February 2016, reported "*Substandard medicines could be three times more prevalent than the government says, two new studies show … Substandard drugs work less effectively, causing the disease to run a longer course, and can even require a new prescription during treatment. Substandard drugs also contribute to antibacterial resistance, a threat that has doubled in the last five years in India.*"

India Spend also reported that about 4.5% of the drugs sold in the Indian market are substandard, according to the studies undertaken by the Central Drug Standard Control Organisation (CDSCO), the official regulatory authority. Reputed brands too fail to meet the quality standards, because many consumers believe these (reputed) products to be better than others.

The 'International medical products anti-counterfeiting taskforce (IMPACT)' of World Health Organization (WHO) defines SFFC medicines as "medicines which are deliberately and fraudulently mislabelled with respect to identity and/or source, and also which may include products with correct ingredients or with the wrong ingredients, without active ingredients, with insufficient or too much active ingredient, or with fake packaging".

As per Khan and Khar[17]:

SFFC drugs are a pandemic threat …

India is considered as the main originator and distributor of SFFC drugs …

India is the largest manufacturer of generic drugs and probably 12-25% of the medicines supplied globally are contaminated, substandard and counterfeit.

"Being the world's largest manufacturers of active pharmaceutical ingredients and finished products, it is likely that India along with China could be the major contributors to spurious medications", as per Patrick Lukulay, vice president of US Pharmacopoeial Convention's global health programs.

In a report, it has been declared by the European Commission that 75% of the global cases of SFFC medicines originate from India.

If the above does not scare you, then what will?

Unfortunately, the problem does not end there. Read on…

1.3.9 Superbugs

We also have a growing problem of Superbugs which are born in India. Most middle class Indians consider themselves as doctors ("DWDs"–*Doctors without Degrees*). People buy antibiotics over the counter and then don't even complete the full course. The bacteria becomes resistant to the drug and stronger in the process. Next time, it needs a stronger drug to get defeated, but that can happen only if the patient takes the full dose and strictly as per a doctor's advice, which does not happen unfortunately.

An online newspaper, *The Wire*, dated 16 January 2017, published an article, titled, "Superbug from India resistant to all known antibiotics." Reportedly, a woman in the US died in September 2016 after being infected by a superbug during her visit to India. She had lived in India for two years and had been hospitalised at least four times for a right femur fracture and a subsequent hip fracture prior

---

17 Khan A N & Khar R K, 2015, *Current Scenario of Spurious and Substandard Medicines in India: A Systematic Review*, Indian Journal of Pharmaceutical Sciences, Indian J Pharm Sci. 2015 Jan-Feb; 77(1): 2–7.

to contracting the Superbug. Her US doctors found that the bacteria was resistant to all available antibiotics. None of the 14 antibiotics that physicians used to treat her worked. The infection was caused by carbapenem-resistant Enterobacteriaceae (CRE), a multidrug-resistant organism associated with high mortality.

She died of septic shock in early September 2016, less than two months after her admission to this US hospital.

To prevent such unfortunate recurrences, antibiotics must be genuine and authentic; of full strength as shown on the package; and strictly sold only through the prescription of a registered medical practitioner. India and the world can't afford Superbugs due to misuse of antibiotics by the Indian people. The concerned government authorities and drug controllers must launch a nationwide campaign to effectively educate people so that they desist from such malpractices. If that does not happen, people in India and the wider world may find themselves pushed back a hundred years into a pre-antibiotic era (i.e. pre-1928). In 1928, Sir Alexander Flaming, a Scottish biologist, discovered the antibiotic substance called *penicillin*.

1.3.10 General Safety & Security Concerns

Many Indians are still very orthodox and conservative in their thoughts and approach to general life, especially towards their women. They openly threaten their women against wearing western clothing, such as a pair of jeans or skirts.

The Indian newspapers are full of stories about the status of Indian women and the crime against women in the country. For foreigners, it is the crime against the women tourists which is of grave concern—as to how safe is one while travelling through India? Even men share some of their own concerns about their personal security.

The foreign tourists come from entirely different cultural and social backgrounds. Most tourists, particularly from western countries, carry a contrastingly different philosophical approach towards life in general, and the way they dress, or carry themselves. But that must not be considered as a reason to justify crime against them. Unfortunately, every now and then, the newspapers are full of stories of many such crimes carried out by the locals against many unsuspecting women tourists, which generally include crimes committed by drivers of auto-rickshaws, buses or taxis, the tourist guide, or a hotel staff. In many cases, their western dress (jeans, shorts, skirts), or the way they talk freely with people are blamed, which is an utter shame. This mindset exposes a contrasting cultural division between an average Indian and a regular foreign tourist, particularly visiting from a western country. It does not matter if the molester himself wears western dress or sports sunglasses or uses social media or speaks a few words of English—the molester is culturally, at heart, a few hundred years behind the world culture. In the developed world, women are not considered objects for personal gratification of men; they enjoy parity with their male counterparts and freedom to do things their own way.

As for unsuspecting male tourists, cases like theft, physical assault and robbery are very common.

The Indian Government's *Atithi Devo Bhava* campaign is certainly a step in the right direction, but culturally orthodox and backward people don't truly understand its spirit and the true meaning. Education is certainly important, but equally important is the strict and timely implementation of legal punishments. It all boils down to a serious educational campaign dedicated to inculcate good moral and social values at the school level, aimed to bring up the general mentality and morality of men in line with their counterparts in the developed world.

1.4 CORRUPTION & WHITE-ANTING ISSUES

One can ask, "Does the country not have rules and regulations and the enforcement authorities to ensure that these issues outlined in this section become non-issues and cease to exist?" The answer is simple: India has everything—a constitution, a parliamentary democracy, rules and regulations. But the enforcement authorities are also Indians and carry the Indian psyche (Ref. Section 1.6).

Like other people, those comprising the enforcement authority also need money to buy a new or a bigger house or a bigger apartment or multiple properties; fund a lavish wedding of their children; pay dowry; meet the constant demands of their life partners, such as buying gold and diamond jewellery; pay for their children's private education (private tutors and private school fees), pay capitation fee in professional colleges for their children receiving tertiary education; fund their adult children's rich lifestyle (electronics, designer clothes, holidays, cars and motorcycles); go for overseas holidays; regular dining out; and fund their personal vices (drinking, gambling, womanising etc.).

Simple mathematical calculations indicate that a government official can't meet all the above expenses with the kind of salary being paid in India. So, it is a culture of '*you scratch my back and I'll scratch yours.*' Enforcement officials generally turn a blind eye to the evils in the country in exchange for receiving favours. The system is such that if you are honest, you will be transferred from your post and sent far away as punishment for causing unnecessary 'strife'. If the person sitting above you is interested in receiving favours, as well as the person reporting to you, you'll have to go with the flow and fit into the system, otherwise you will be removed like a thorn is removed from the flesh. Such is the state of corruption in India[18].

It can be likened to a full blown cancer in the body. In such a state, the body needs both chemotherapy and radiation.

Recently, during a wedding reception dinner in Perth, which was attended by nearly three dozen ex-Indian army, air force and naval officers and their families, I had a long chat with a visiting ex-Indian army officer about current issues confronting the nation. He saw the Kashmir situation as a serious and nagging problem, which is bleeding India and must be effectively and conclusively dealt with as early as

---

18 The online version of *Times of India*, dated 7 March 2017, published an article titled, "India has highest bribery rate among 16 Asia Pacific countries—Transparency International". The newspaper reported 70% Indians paid a bribe when they accessed public services. (In comparison, in Japan, which is the least corrupt country, only 0.2% of the respondents reported paying a bribe.)In India, more than 40% of the respondents felt corruption had increased over the past 12 months. Nearly 73% of those who paid a bribe were from the poorer section of the society. Nearly 59% bribery incidents were reported with procuring government healthcare services and identification related documents. Nearly 58% respondents paid bribes for education.

possible. He wished the Indian army had a relatively freer hand to deal with the situation in Kashmir. He was confident that the Indian army, being one of most disciplined and humanitarian armies in the world, would definitely be able to apply a genuine and everlasting healing touch to the local Kashmiri people and help them to prosper and live in relative peace. He was also not happy that the erstwhile governments in India had not acceded to a long pending request from the forces that the retired army personnel and their families be settled along the border areas with China, similar to what China has reportedly done along the Tibet border. As for the corruption in the country, he blamed the politicians and bureaucracy for it, especially a strong nexus between IAS and IPS officers and their '*you scratch my back and I'll scratch yours*' mantra. He agreed that it was only up to the youth of the country to eradicate the growing menace of corrupt practices in the country, which had grown to cancerous proportions. But he was hopeful that the current government would be able to put a lid on corruption. He expressed full faith in the country's current Prime Minister, Mr Modi.

Despite the highlights and hallmarks of the country summarised previously in Section 1.2 and the ground reality in Section 1.3, it is sad to see that not many Indian people, from all walks of life, are aware that their country is under a potential threat from the following white-anting issues, which will potentially make it very difficult for their future generations to thrive.

- Alarming rate of population growth
  - Worsening air quality
  - Fast dwindling availability of clean drinking water
  - Increasing traffic and numerous related issues, e.g. harmful emissions, noise pollution, and adverse effects on human time and health
  - Food adulteration
  - Toxic groundwater (with heavy metals and arsenic) that affects the crops and, therefore, the human health
- The general Indian mindset
  - A rat race, with a reduced trust factor
  - Diluted social values

    - A clear shift from the traditional, simpler and spiritualistic lifestyle to a more complex, competitive and materialistic lifestyle
- The middle and upper class consumerism
    - Feeds corruption at all levels to support a growing affluent lifestyle
    - Increases the overall carbon footprint and pollution level in the country
- Regional politics, caste system and potential inter-religious issues
    - Affect harmony and trust amongst the fellow citizens
    - Non-homogeneity and disunity affects the country's morale, progress, security and sovereignty
    - Promotes regionalism and potentially weakens the bond that provides the basis for a unified country and a national identity.

1.5 ALARMING POPULATION GROWTH

The following statistics[19] are absolutely shocking:

- Current population–1 339 094 331 (i.e. about 1.34 billion)
- Current male population (51.6%)–691 409 758 (i.e. about 691 million)
- Current female population (48.4%)–647 684 573 (i.e. about 648 million)
- Births this year–4 705 951 (i.e. about 4.7 million)
- Births today–42 241
- Deaths this year–1 708 530 (i.e. about 1.7 million)
- Deaths today–15 336
- Net migration this year– (-) 94 534
- Net migration today–(-) 849
- Population growth this year–2 902 887 (i.e. about 2.9 million)
- Population growth today–26 057 (i.e. about 26 thousand since this morning)

---

19 As per http://countrymeters.info/en/India at 1.54 pm (AWST) on 6 March 2017.

It is alarming to see that, with each hour, India has a net increase of about two thousand people in her population, i.e. a net increase of about 48 thousand people every day. The current birth to death ratio is 2.76. During 2017, the Indian population is projected to increase by about 17 million. The daily change rates are projected to be as follows:

- About 75 thousand live births on average per day (i.e. about 3,110 people per hour)
- About 27 thousand deaths on average per day (i.e. about 1,130 people per hour)
- And about 1,500 people leaving the country on average per day (i.e. about 63 people leave the country every hour)

The Indian population is projected to reach 1.35 billion by the start of 2018.

For a comparison, the current total Australian population is around 22.8 million people and the birth to death ratio is 1.74. This means, for every one person dying, India adds an additional one human being to its population as compared to Australia.

It is not very difficult to see how a booming population growth in India has, and shall, continue to impact upon the overall quality of life of all Indians. Given that the land area is constant and the natural resources are not unlimited, the quality of life will keep thinning out as time goes by.

The population growth has a flow-on effect on the overall environment in the country, including the quality of air, water, water bodies, groundwater and food, all of which seem to deteriorate with time.

The country's energy requirement will keep increasing with each day, especially as the people keep becoming relatively more affluent, due to the country's current fast economic growth. The ever increasing demand for more power (electricity) will continue to put a significant pressure on the generation, transmission and supply of electricity. With each day and seemingly a growing affluence, more and more people will make use of air-conditioners, refrigerators, common cooking appliances and other entertainment facilities at home, which will keep increasing the demand for more electricity.

The increasing demand for domestic power supply will also be exacerbated due to the climate change, which the world seems to be undergoing at the present, with India tipped to become hotter with time, as indicated by the historical meteorological data. In addition, the effect of vehicular and industrial emissions will keep intensifying the greenhouse effect, trapping the heat closer to the ground which, in turn, will exacerbate an already growing demand for air-conditioners and refrigerators.

Unless the power generation is renewable (hydel, solar, wind or tidal) or nuclear, a looming much higher consumption of fossil fuels (diesel and coal) will keep polluting the environment to very significant levels.

Some important questions that must be answered:

- Can India sustain the current population growth? Most likely not!
- How is she going to feed all those additional mouths when already a considerable number of poor people are starving? An impossible task!
- Are the natural resources and the sources of food showing a corresponding increase with the increase in population? Certainly not!
- Is the agriculture land growing in size corresponding to an increase in population? Certainly not!
- Is the land for residential development growing in size corresponding to an increase in population? Certainly not!
- Are the automobiles on Indian roads growing in number corresponding to an increase in the population? Yes, every day, Indian roads add about 54 thousand vehicles.
- Does fresh milk production increase in proportion to an increase in population, i.e. are the current dairies in India able to meet the demand to feed 48 thousand new babies (or their mothers) every day? Certainly not! The percentage of adulterated milk is likely to keep increasing further from the current 68% to meet the growing new demand every day.

As per a World Bank report, dated 27 May 2016, about 22% of the Indian population (i.e. 270 million) lives below the poverty line.

That is one out of five Indians is poor. Also, about 80% of India's poor live in rural areas where the development is scanty and people produce more children to do labour and help the household with some income to survive.

Public speaking about the (alarming) population growth may possibly be a taboo in India. Interestingly, India gave the world the inverted Red Triangle[20] for family planning decades ago, but that triangle seems to have disappeared over time. In my childhood, there used to be a slogan written (in Hindi) on virtually every wall of the country: '*Do ya teen bachee hote hain ghar main ache*', which meant '*two to three children are ideal for a family*'. As India's population crossed the 60 crore mark, the government got concerned and dropped one child from the slogan and replaced it with a new slogan: '*hum do hamare do*' (meaning '*we two, our two*'). However, in a few years when the population suddenly reached the 100 crore mark, one more child was dropped from the slogan and it was replaced by a new slogan: '*Hum do hamara ek*' (meaning 'we two, our one') in support of a one-child policy. Now, all these slogans have become invisible, seemingly gone missing surreptitiously. Although, in India, many people whinge about the population issue, yet there seems to be is no political debate on it. One may conclude that such a debate has become taboo in India, as it may cause serious political harm to any political party which tries to raise and promote it.

Interestingly, the people I know in India, especially the young professionals, have generally one child, with two children in rare cases. And some couples choose to have no child at all. These professionals work and live in the cities of India.

So, an important question arises: Where are these new 2,000 children arriving from every minute of the day? Of course, India

---

[20] An inverted Red Triangle is the symbol for family planning health and contraception services. It is believed to have been invented by Deep Tyagi, an Indian family planning official and activist in the 1960s. It is still prevalent in many developing nations such as Ghana, Gambia, Zimbabwe, Egypt and Thailand, where it can be seen outside shops and clinics that offer family planning products, as well as commercial and government messages that promote reproductive health services and population control.

is a populated country. One must not do the population maths in percentages, because that would be misleading. This mathematics must involve actual numbers.

As that doctor broke the sad news of my mother's illness to me, without any fear or bias or without using a sweetener, the truth must be told. Indians must face this truth—the country can't afford to have any more new citizens; she is bursting at her seams; she is crying; she can't breastfeed any more children. Enough is enough! Give her rest and let her recover for a while. At least, get her birth rate equal or preferably lower than her death rate, so that the net population growth is zero or preferably negative for a decade or so. Please—Is anyone listening out there?

In India, everything has a political connotation. Negative politics is the order of the day. Interestingly, India still claims to have parliamentary democracy! But, out of ignorance or perhaps malice, every opposition party plays a negative role, instead of being constructive. I call it '*compulsive negativism disorder*'. Everyone wants to rule the country. That is fine, but with what intention? Stitch her seams or further cut them loose? Is the role of a political party only meant to use sweeteners, adopt divisive politics and mislead people with blatant lies and half-truths, by way of simply exploiting their illiteracy and ignorance, so as to come into power at the time of the next elections? Is that what (Indian) democracy is all about?

In contrast, it is not hard to look at China, especially how that country has addressed its population issue. But that is another matter! One may say China has a different system of governance and a political system. Reportedly, the Chinese governance is in the hands of many engineers. Can the Indians strive and succeed to achieve similar outcomes through democratic means? Where is the prudence?

Recently, over phone, I discussed the looming population issues of India with my father and uncle at Jammu. Both are retired Chief Engineers from the J &K government service. To my surprise, they did not think the growing population was such a big issue in India.

My uncle advised, "Well, we humans are gifted by God with a fertile brain. We must use our brain and produce all that we need to sustain and thrive from our land. We must develop super food, which can be consumed in much lesser quantity and still be able to give us the required energy and all nutrients."

I replied, "Uncle, your house has ten rooms. Ideally, at one time, your house should be able to accommodate not more than 16 people, leaving out the kitchen and bathrooms from being used as bedrooms. However, if you have to accommodate 16 more people, such as in the case of an emergency, you may still be able to do that, but every room will now be used by more than two people. However, if 50 more people are to be accommodated in your house, you may have no option but to allow them to sleep on the floor in bathrooms, kitchen and the corridors, and also on the roof top. In a nutshell, your house can't keep on accommodating more and more people; there must be an upper limit to ensure a reasonable quality of life is available to all people who live there. Our country is also like your house. There must be an upper limit in her population; she can't keep on producing more and more. What is that number? Can anyone answer this question?

"Uncle, I have heard about a book which was published about ten years back or so. It was about '*human plague*'. In that book, the author is reported to have used established scientific and philosophical tools, and mathematics, and predicted that the world population would keep on growing till it reached about 9.5 billion (currently it is about 7.4 billion and still growing). At that point, due to a range of adverse human activities, similar to how rats contribute to plague, something very bad would happen and the human population in the world would suddenly crash to about 3.5 billion, which may then become more sustainable."

My uncle had no answer. He changed the topic of conversation. I am not sure if he was really convinced with my view and my deep apprehensions. Perhaps not! History will tell, in due course. Most educated people agree with me that the current Indian population growth is a big issue, but do not necessarily agree with me that it is '*the issue*'. Many simply shrug their shoulders and say, "What can we do?" I refuse to accept this helpless attitude. I pray the youth of India wake up to this stark realisation and start a campaign to convince people, especially the poor, not to produce more.

It would not be unreasonable to look at the country's airports as barometers for gauging the country's growth in terms of her pollution, affordability and affluence. The international and domestic airports at Delhi and Mumbai have not long ago been upgraded to international standards. Both airports are very impressive in terms of size and facilities. But the question is how long will they suffice given the pressure they will keep experiencing with each day from a growing middle class in a country which is currently the fastest growing economy in the world.

On 17 March 2017, *The Times of India* published an article, titled, '*IGI Choked: No new peak-hour flights in Delhi this summer*'.

The newspaper reported, "*Indians may be flying like never before but the infrastructure crunch at metro airports is limiting their choice of flights. The problem is so acute that putting an additional flight in peak hours is becoming tough at most metros. Airlines are pleading with Mumbai airport to allow more domestic flights at night as the airport has no additional slots left. These two airports alone account for almost 10 crore of the total (domestic-cum-international) traffic of just over 15 crore last year. The severe infrastructure crunch at major Indian airports was highlighted during recent deliberations the aviation authorities held with airlines to finalise the summer schedule this year.*"

There is an old saying in India, "*Jitni chadar, utne paon failao,*" which means in English "*Cut your cloth according to your size.*" There is no doubt India is experiencing a boom in infrastructure development, as one can easily see numerous construction works being undertaken in all cities in the form of new flyovers, roads, buildings etc. But all those works take their own time to be completed; construction does not happen overnight. By the time these structures are commissioned, the population has already surged ahead. So, whatever is being constructed now will always potentially fall short of the growing demands at a future date. And, one must remember, there is always a limit, in terms of the actual availability of land and the site access, for undertaking such infrastructure development works. India can't perennially be constructing new bridges and flyovers and expanding roads in her cities; it must stop somewhere, otherwise road blockages to allow construction works, and the resulting traffic jams will keep making city living and road driving a continued nightmarish experience. Instead, such essential infrastructure development works must be extended to the villages and other remote and inaccessible areas of the country, so that people don't have to migrate to the cities. Such developmental extension works will also provide sources of earning livelihood to the local people in those villages and remote areas. The whole country must develop uniformly; and the cities must be spared any further growth to allow the city people to breathe.

Empowering all girls and women in the country could be the key to a possible deceleration in the current population growth rate. If all females, not only in the cities but in all villages (where 75% population of India lives), receive education and employment, they will gradually cease to be exploited by their males and older orthodox uneducated women. Therefore, to some extent, disempowerment of men, through education and employment of women, is necessary so that men no longer use their women as slaves for undertaking only the basic household chores and the child production work. Once all women are educated and employed, they will resist their men against having more children, as is already happening in the western world and more developed countries. Education and employment will not only liberate a woman from the traditional bondages of her home and multiple child births, but will also restore her inherent dignity and parity with a man. She will feel safer. The country will also benefit due to a bigger workforce.

When half of her population is empowered, Mother India will truly smile.

1.6 TYPICAL INDIAN PSYCHE

In a general way, the average Indian mindset has its roots lying deep in the cultural philosophy of the country. It only got distorted due to adulteration caused by materialism. Goddess Saraswati (the goddess of art and knowledge) has more or less now been dethroned and replaced by Goddess Laxmi (the goddess of wealth and prosperity).

India, in particular, holds a conservative approach towards many issues unlike western countries and also has a tendency of taking things for granted, be it a matter of cleanliness or crime—nobody seems bothered. The morality is designed on the basis of the society to which an individual belongs. In general terms, Indians demonstrate a hypocritical approach and double standards with regard to their views on women, religion, and culture.

A general interaction with an average middle class Indian reflects a strange and outdated psyche that obviously has a toxic effect on the very foundations of the nation. The nation seems to be confused between traditional old-world values, spirituality, and the new-world materialism and consumerism. Everyone seems to be in a rush and in a kind of rat race. The question is: To what end, eventually?

Before moving further, it is important to understand the typical Indian psyche in order to know the reason underlying the state of affairs in India. The following provides an insight into how Indians generally think about a range of mundane issues and everyday matters:

Definition of a Superior Product

A superior product or a superior design means something new in the market; should be a little complex and not easy for people to understand; should have a glittering look and, of course, must look expensive and branded. Recently, a very senior government official in the educational system of India boasted in front of a visiting Australian academic delegation, "We have very good quality books in India, but teachers can't teach from them, as the concepts are very complex." The two members of the Australian team looked at each other and wondered at this paradoxical statement. They wondered how things can be of a 'very good quality' and 'complex' at the same time. Any product or concept which is complex can't be described as being of very good quality. In the western world, the quality of a product or a concept is judged by the simplicity with which it can be used, understood or explained, respectively.

Big is Better

The bigger the better it is, whether it is the house or the main gate of the house, the car, television or the refrigerator.

You should look bigger and more prosperous than others, otherwise what have you achieved? People think their social respect and standing lies in the size of their assets. They identify themselves with their materialistic progress. So, their focus remains on the accumulation of bigger and better assets instead of their own self.

Money Talks and Walks

Money is everything—the more one has, the lesser it is. As a matter of fact, many people live a lifestyle which sends a message that wealth is considered more important than health. Most people pray to the Hindu Goddess of wealth, Laxmi, instead of the Goddess of knowledge, Saraswati. In my growing years in Kashmir, our elders would hold Saraswati higher than Laxmi based on a wise logic—if Saraswati is happy with you, Laxmi will follow, which means if one has the right education and knowledge, one can always make money. However, in the past 25 years, since their migration from Kashmir, the Pandits of Kashmir, under influence from the rest of the Indians, have reversed the status and the importance of the two Goddesses. An Indian friend once advised me that we should keep a picture of Laxmi (depicted in a sitting posture, rather than standing) facing the main entry of the house in order to accumulate wealth. He said, "a standing Laxmi allows the money to leave the house."

Indians have a general tendency to show off their wealth, be it through their status, assets or weddings. This tendency is fast feeding and fuelling the growing consumerism and corruption, and in the process eroding the traditional human values and sincerity in social interactions.

For some bizarre reason, most Indians judge progress by individual wealth and assets rather than by the quality of life and virtues. Being rich becomes an end in itself. It is not very uncommon to hear many people boasting about the high salary of their friend or relative in India, or their own assets. Many say, "India is not the same country that you know; it is changing. People earn in crores now." My general response to such comments is, "Fair enough, it is encouraging to hear that. But, do you know the typical median salary of middle class is less than Rupees 60,000 per month, and middle class forms the bulk of the Indian population? What percentage of the Indian population does earn the kind of money that you are talking about?" India is still a poor country[21]. Even if a person is able to earn crores of rupees, he shall still have to breathe the same polluted air, drink the same toxic water, and move on the same choked roads through the same chaotic traffic. One may try to live in an air-conditioned environment, but how long? And, someone has to pay for air-conditioning—moneywise and through environmental degradation. To generate power, you have to burn fossil fuels and the whole country suffers due to environmental pollution.

Gold Glitters

Indians love to buy and wear gold; most of the gold is imported from Australia and South Africa. Most of the gold ornaments generally remain hidden away from the eyes of burglars in bank lockers, as people are afraid of potential burglaries and risk to their lives in the process. Artificial jewellery and artificial gold, or anything that glitters, is usually used on a daily basis. But, in any case, jewellery must be worn and it should glitter. These days, unlike their forefathers, many men also wear broad and thick golden bracelets, thick gold chains and rings; some wear rings studded with diamonds on all four fingers of either hand.

Branded & Designer

Indians love branded clothes. The upper middle class people go to Dubai, Bangkok or Singapore to do their shopping. They look for a designer's mark and brand on your shirt, watch, trousers, jumpers or shoes to judge how expensive it is and, indirectly, how well you are doing in your life. It is all about show and showing-off. Things must look 'expensive' to impress people.

In the seventies, with a similar mindset, people used to look down upon cotton shirts because cotton was cheaper than synthetic material (Terylene) at that time. The trend has now reversed and cotton rules

---

[21] As Global Finance, out of 189 countries, India ranks 126th ($6,658) amongst world's wealthiest countries as measured by GDP per capita, adjusted for purchasing power parity (PPP) in 2016. By comparison, China is 81st ($15,423) and Pakistan is 137th ($5,120).

these days. Now poorer people generally wear synthetic material more than the rich.

And, where is that designer's logo? If you don't have one to show off, your shirt, jacket, trousers, shoes, sunglasses, handbags have no value.

Donation & Bribery

Indians love to donate gold and money to their deities at the temple, perhaps as bribe to God, rather than donate their wealth to charity, which would help millions of disadvantaged people and a range of just causes.

If people truly believed the omnipresence of God, and the true meaning of *namaskar*, they would try to please God by serving humans. Recently, the chief minister of a southern state of India donated gold worth millions of rupees to a certain temple and fulfilled his vow. It was national news in India. Did anyone ask him how he managed to fund this donation?

A child is taught at a very young age by his elders how to ask for favours from God at a temple in exchange for a small donation of money. At a place of worship, many parents can be seen giving some money to their child for passing it on to the priest, with instructions, '*Bhagwan ji ko paisa do and apne liye kuchh maango*', (Give the money to God and ask for anything in return for yourself). The child is, thus, inducted into this practice for the rest of his life. It becomes a way of life for him.

Tall Poppy—We are the Best

Born out of a stiff competition, due to the growing population and inherent human jealousy, many Indians desire there should be no one better than them or their children—in status, beauty, education or wealth.

Many Indians believe the Indian education system is better than the rest of the world. Their perception is due to a high emigration rate of Indian students and professionals to other countries. Many Indians, living overseas, also believe the Indian education system is much better than that of their respective countries of residence. Their perception is based on (a) a much smaller size of the school bag that their child has to carry to school in their country of residence; (b) no encouragement for rote learning; (c) not much home work; and (d) a high approachability and friendliness of the school staff. They believe, as in India, the school staff should not be very friendly; the teacher should look very stern and the school principal should be unapproachable. They also believe the school bag should be as heavy as it is in India and the child should be busy with tonnes of home work and no life after school.

The Times of India, dated 15 September 2015, referring to the QS World University Rankings 2015/16 of Indian Institutions, reported, *"Two Indian institutes have, for the first time, made it to the top 200 list of the world's best universities. The Indian Institute of Science, Bengaluru, has taken the top spot among its Indian counterparts, bagging the 147th rank. The only other Indian institute to make it to the top 200 is Indian Institute of Technology, Delhi, ranked 179th this year. It has made great progress from last year when it was ranked 235th in the world."*

In comparison, in 2016, eight Australian universities figured in the top 125 universities[22], of which six were rated in the top 65 universities, with Australian National University (ANU) leading at No 22 in the world. I haven't heard any Australian academic saying that we are the best. In Australia, most people are relatively humble and admit that we have the scope to improve further and be better than we are. It is noteworthy that India adds about 17 million annually to her population, which is not far from the entire population of Australia.

Authority & Hierarchy

Indians enjoy positions of authority and power, and continuously work to climb the power ladder. Authority over others feeds their ego. Recently, I overhead a gentleman from India asking his young niece, a fresh graduate, over phone, "How many people report to you?" She smiled and said, "I have just started; no one reports to me. Is that important?" In Australia, organisational structures are more lateral than vertical—matrix systems.

---

22 Ref. QS World University Rankings -http://www.australianuniversities.com.au/rankings/

To judge another person's social status, many Indians carry an intrinsic curiosity about how much the other person earns. Questions like, "Which suburb do you live in; which car do you drive; where do you shop; and where did you go for holidays last year?" are common with Indians. During those earlier years in the mid-nineties, after I went overseas to work and live, some people would even ask me, shamelessly, "What is your salary?" I would dodge the question tactfully. But, even then, one day a 'polished' gentleman asked me, "What is the level of salary that professionals like you earn there." I provided him with a very wide range of salaries to keep guessing. With time, such curious people have stopped bothering me. But their x-ray eyes keep scanning me and my attire closely—my shoes, watch etc. Recently, one gentleman excitedly remarked, "Ha, you are still wearing the same watch that you wore when you were a student."He must have deduced that I was not doing very well in my life. But that is a good deduction, I think. It works for me. At least he will not bother me now.

The *Mainu Ki* Attitude

In English, the *Mainu ki* attitude (Punjabi) may mean a '*devil-may-care*' attitude or literally '*not my concern*' in regard to general social and public matters. It is a common view in India, especially Jammu and Delhi, that most of the household trash is thrown by people outside their main door. People throw banana skins, orange peels and peanut shells wherever they want without any care or awareness. People urinate and defecate openly in streets, open areas, along railways tracks and wherever they can. Prime Minister, Mr Modi, has tried to address the issue after understanding the underlying Indian psyche. He virtually started his term as the country's Prime Minister with a 'Clean India' campaign and a slogan known popularly as *Swachh Bharat Abhiyan*[23].

[23] Means 'Clean India Movement'—it is a campaign launched by Prime Minister Modi in 2014 on Mahatma Gandhi's birth anniversary (2 October) at Rajghat, to clean the country's streets, roads and infrastructure. It is believed to be India's largest ever cleanliness drive, with 3 million government employees, and school and college students from all parts of India participating in the campaign. The objectives are to reduce or eliminate open defecation through construction of individual, cluster and community toilets, and also establishan accountable mechanism of monitoring latrine use in India.

Now it is up to the people to understand his concern and follow his message in letter and spirit.

Snobbish is Cool

To be snobbish and condescending is considered cool. Similar to the French language, in the Hindi language also, 'you' can be used in two ways—the word '*aap*' is used when you speak with your boss, teacher, superior or senior, an older or a powerful person—politically, rich or a professional of higher standing. However, when speaking to a junior person, a subordinate, or a servant, people generally use the word '*tu*' or '*tum*'. So, there is a clear discrimination in the way Hindi speaking people speak to other people. Generally, people don't speak 'with' another person; they speak 'to' another person.

Gender Bias

The general cross-section of the Indian society is widely known to show a strong cultural gender bias against females, with males enjoying a blanket superiority over their female counterparts. It is very much entrenched in the Indian DNA and it all starts from the home. In many cases, it starts from the mother herself! Why? Because she does not want her girl child to suffer like other women due to general societal prejudice and bias. She also gets worried about the dowry that she would have to save and offer for her newborn baby girl's wedding after maybe 20 years.

It all starts right from the moment a female child is born. Unfortunately, in the recent years, many parents try to know the gender of the foetus in advance of baby's birth, which results in many female foeticides. This has resulted in males outnumbering females. As per an estimate[24]:

- On 31 December 2106, India had a male population of about 670 million, with only about 646 million females. That meant males outnumbered females in India by about 24 million, which is almost the entire population of Australia.

---

[24] http://countrymeters.info/en/India

- As of 1 January 2017, the sex ratio of the total population was 1.068 (i.e. 1,068 males per 1,000 females), which was higher than the global sex ratio of 1.016.
- Based on a 2011 Census data, an online newspaper, *FIRSTPOST*, dated 30 April 2013, published an article, titled '*Haryana worst in sex ratio, a 2011 Census find*', which presented the following alarming figures:
  - The worst five performing states in terms of female to male ratio were headed by Haryana, where the number of females per 1000 males stood at 879; followed by Jammu and Kashmir (889 females), Punjab (895 females), Uttar Pradesh (912 females) and Bihar (918 females). Interestingly, all these are northern states of India.
  - The top five performing states were Kerala (1,084 females), Tamil Nadu (996), Andhra Pradesh (993), Chhattisgarh (991) and Odisha (979). Interestingly, all these are southern states of India.
  - The male child (0 to 6 years) population had increased whereas female child population had decreased during the 2001 to 2011 period. The worst performing states in this age group were Haryana (834 females), Punjab (846), Jammu and Kashmir (862), Rajasthan (888) and Gujarat (890).

On 16 March 2017, *The Times of India* published an article, titled "Maharashtra sees decline in sex ratio." The newspaper reported: "*In a disturbing trend indicative of a strong male bias, Maharashtra has recorded a dismal child sex ratio of 899 girls per 1,000 boys, according to the Family Planning department statistics released on Thursday. Maharashtra's performance has dropped significantly from the 2001 census, when it had 913 girls per 1,000 boys. Incidentally, the national average of 914 is also the worst India has had since Independence.*"

The newspaper reported sickening news of police arresting a 42 year old homeopath in connection with the "death of a pregnant woman during an abortion at his hospital and the subsequent recovery of 19 aborted foetuses wrapped in polythene bags near a stream in the village."

Quoting experts, the newspaper also reported: "The drop in Maharashtra over the past decade is frightening and speaks of the overall neglect of girl children. A closer look reveals that nearly 4.69 lakh girls are 'missing' in the state, which shows that Maharashtra has not taken the practice of fighting sex determination seriously."

The above findings clearly show a north-south cultural divide in the country. The statistics are a clear reflection of a sickening practice of female foeticide in some parts of India. Ironically, people in these states widely pray to various forms of Mother Goddess—Durga, Laxmi, Saraswati, Vaishno Devi, Jwala Devi. In these states, it is a fashion to organise *jagran,* which means performing nightlong prayers and traditional rituals dedicated to Mother Goddess.

During a *jagran*, the main singers of the professional organisers(on a loudspeaker), all members of the host family, and all other attendees continuously shout through the whole night, "*Jai Mata Di*", which means "*Hail the Mother*" or "*Victory to the Mother*". I know a rich businessman at Delhi, who in his younger days would organise *jagrans* at his home every now and then, and reward his relatives on giving birth to male children. Obviously, he is one of those naïve people who has never understood the concept of Mother Nature.

In addition, one must see the rush of pilgrims visiting various shrines of Mother Goddess, such as Vaishno Devi, throughout the year. What does it all mean? Female foeticide, dowry and dowry deaths! Hypocrisy or half-baked faith and poor understanding. Simply unbelievable! Well, that is India! She needs a serious educational campaign to save the girl child; it seems the concept of Mother Goddess is not enough.

It is shameful that people can't see their Mother Goddess in their own mothers, grandmothers, aunts, sisters, daughters, wives, female colleagues and any woman out there. Aren't all these women part of the same creation. Haven't they created or don't they create or will they not continue to create and nurture human race. Can this world exist without a woman? Can a man conceive and carry a baby for nine months?

Do people really understand the God concept? I think that is not the right question. The question should rather be, "How many people really understand the God concept?" And the next question would be, "Those who understand the God concept, how can they differentiate between God and the real people? Also, how can one expect those who don't understand the God concept not to differentiate between the real people and God?" I think the country needs to revisit the God concept and not only try to look for God within the four walls of their places of worship. God can't be confined to those man-made structures. God is everywhere, within everything, within every being! That is the reason underlying the traditional Indian greeting—*namaskar.* People fold their hands, bow their head a little, close their eyes and humbly utter the word *namaskar* to the other person, which in layman's language means, "*I bow unto the God residing within you*". Indians must revisit their traditional greeting and extend that to the real world. Then only, they will understand the omnipresence of God and, logically and hopefully, break a disconnect between Mother Goddess and the women they see around. Nearly half of India's population is female. Treat them as equals.

Indian women must regain their parity with their male counterparts, which they perhaps enjoyed once before the religion was born. They must empower themselves by educating themselves and helping millions like them to get education. Power is not given; power is taken.

Women have proved around the world that they are no less than males in any walk of life; there is no need for them to prove anything more to anyone. In fact, they are superior to the men in many aspects of life. It is time that a paradigm shift is forced through the Indian community, in theory and through practice, and a change in the mindset of orthodox and religious minded Indians is accelerated to make up for the lost time. It is 2017. The world can't anymore afford all those outdated and baseless notions about the male superiority. Males can't survive on their own; they are only a part of the creation.

Why can't people understand the relevance of *Navratri* festival—the nine auspicious days of fasting and celebrations in India, especially the northern part of India, that are devoted every year to the nine forms of Mother Goddess? Those nine forms of Mother Goddess are the reminder of the Mothers' capability and her real power. Is there any equivalent festival in India dedicated to Father God? Perhaps no! So, why should we not think and understand the message about the power within the female gender?

Till the moment a child is born, most family members, relatives and friends hold their breath and pray for a male child. People are extremely curious to know the sex of the child. They virtually run to congratulate the parents and one another as soon as it is announced that a male child is born; some start dancing in the home or out in the street, wherever they are, and sweets are distributed around. Many family members immediately rush to shrines and temples to thank their deity. However, if the news is that a baby girl is born, a strange deathly hush sweeps the environment. Not to speak of sweets, offering simple greetings to the mother is also a taboo. The poor mother is even scared to look into the eyes of her mother-in-law, her husband or sister-n-law, as if she has committed a serious crime by giving birth to a female child.

For a range of reasons, even in this day and age, a considerable percentage of educated females, and their mothers and mothers-in-law, would prefer to have their first born as a male child, although they may not mind having their second child a female to complete the family. As an involuntary wish, by default, a significant percentage of elders and parents bless their daughter with, "May you be blessed with a *beta/putra* (a son)!" This general attitude in favour of male children indirectly encourages and emboldens young males to carry out a range of indecent activities towards females. It also undermines the confidence and a sense of security amongst women, with the result a vast majority of females grow up with a sickening sense of over-dependence on their male counterparts, losing their personal freedom of thought and action in the process. Do they know this world was not possible without females? Furthermore, science has proven that females are better than males biologically and emotionally. The current world has also seen that females, if given the chance, prove to be no less than males in many traditional male-centric professions, such as law, engineering, academics, sports and defence (army, air force and navy), and so many other professions. Traditionally, in India, a daughter used to be considered as *Parayadhan* (*property of others*).

I am not very sure to what extent this thought is still carried in India. Also, I am not sure about the origin of this thought—is it societal, cultural or religious? It is paradoxical to see that, in a country where a goddess is widely worshipped, as Saraswati, Laxmi or Durga, a girl child has traditionally enjoyed an inferior status. Is that due to a traditional dowry culture, which is still prevalent in many parts of India; or the religious dogmas and taboos; or due to a relatively smaller physical structure (weight, height and strength) of the females as compared to their male counterparts, or due to a combination of all these? Well, in this day and age, it is not important to know the reasons behind such thought; what is important is that such a thought must now be truly nipped in the bud. We are living in a scientific age, and not in dark ages.

Every year, 8 March is celebrated as International Women's Day (IWD). In 2017, the campaign theme has been *Be Bold for Change*. There was a call to the masses to help forge a better working world, a more gender inclusive world.

In 2016, the campaign theme was *Pledge for Parity*. The day was dedicated to help women and girls achieve their ambitions; challenge conscious and unconscious bias; call for gender-balanced leadership; value women and men's contributions equally; and create inclusive flexible cultures. But the World Economic Forum predicts the gender gap won't close entirely until 2186, which is still 170 years away. Can one wait that long?

IWD is an important catalyst and vehicle for driving greater change for women and moving closer to gender parity.

Each one of us—woman, man or non-binary—can be a leader within our own spheres of influence by taking bold pragmatic action to accelerate gender parity. Through purposeful collaboration, we can together help women advance and unleash the limitless potential offered to economies around the world.

The Australian Prime Minister, Malcolm Turnbull, marked this occasion in 2017 with a strong speech in the Australian parliament. The following is an excerpt from that speech, which sums it all:

"I am delighted to be here at the UN Women Australia's Breakfast and thank you ... the theme today is, 'Empower a woman, empower a nation'... It's a good theme but it should be much more than a theme. It should be absolutely part of our national purpose, our national DNA. When a woman is empowered, the whole economy, the whole community benefits.

Gender equality is not just an issue for women. It is the responsibility of all Australians, of all citizens, here and around the world, because all benefit...Now the empowerment of women is the most powerful tool at the disposal of any government to keep communities strong and the economy resilient...We want more women employed as researchers, innovators, and entrepreneurs, and reaching leadership positions in all sectors of society.

And role models, many of whom are here today, are so important.

Disrespecting women does not always result in violence against women. But all violence against women begins with disrespecting women. That is a fact.

So we can all make a difference. We can be better role models, raising our sons, as Lucy has always said, to have respect for women, beginning with their mothers and their sisters... Raising our daughters to have greater self-esteem.

This cultural shift will take time. Our national "Stop it at the Start" advertising campaign has been a good way to drive that shift.

We are all striving for a society in which women are respected, and are on an absolutely equal footing with men, sharing equally in the corridors of power in politics and business as well as in every room in the home.

As I've said before, gender equality is an economic and social priority for Australia. It's good for women, for families, for business and the economy. It is more than a theme. It should be part of us.

By working together, we can create a society in which women are respected, represented, have a strong voice, are financially and economically secure, and are safe from violence."

Further to Mr Turnbull's speech, I would not like to add anything. He has sent a strong message not only to Australians but to the wider world community, which includes India. After all, we all live in a global village.

The Economic Times, dated 30 June 2015, published an article, titled "*Literacy Rate at 71% in rural India, 86% in urban: Survey*", which reported that male literacy in India was higher than female literacy. Amongst the age group of seven years and above, the male literacy rate was registered at 83%, as compared to 67% for females. In rural areas, 4.5% males and 2.2% females completed the graduation level education and above. In urban areas, the rate was 17% and 13% for males and females, respectively.

It does not mean that women have to now target men to prove their superiority. We must remember that 'one extreme gives birth to another extreme'; so caution is required. Women must empower themselves through knowledge and education, and gain enough confidence to undertake any task; and never hold themselves back or hesitate. There is always a first time.

Mr Modi, the Indian Prime Minister's, slogan "*Beti Bachao, Beti padhao*" ("*save the girl child and educate her*") is a timely reminder to the people of India about what they must do to eradicate the sickening disparity between the two genders. His slogan and the campaign will undoubtedly help to empower the traditionally disadvantaged female gender through their education. Education brings knowledge and knowledge empowers us. If women are empowered, the whole country will flourish.

It is not the stick or a sword or a gun which is mighty; it is, and has been, and will always be, the pen. Brains always rule, and not the muscle! Give the girl child a pen. She may not have as much muscle as her male counterpart, but she has an equally good, perhaps much better brain. She will undoubtedly make this world a better place. She also has love and compassion and will nourish the world with her care.

Thanks to the male ego and his anger, humans have created enough weapons of mass destruction to destroy our planet many times over. We are the only life species on the earth who have created all means of our own self-destruction. Our history bears testimony to this claim. All news channels and newspapers are full of news of hatred, violence and death on a daily basis. Let there be now a transfer of power from the males to their female counterparts if the world is to survive, if love has to grow and we have to continue living as humans beings and not transform over time into barbaric animals or humanoids.

In 2016/2107, India and Australia have one thing in common—the Foreign Ministers of both countries are women—Ms Sushma Swaraj and Ms Julie Bishop—both are exceptionally talented and passionate about their country and their work; both bring human compassion into their work and perform an exemplary role. India and Australia have both had female Prime Ministers in the past—Mrs Indira Gandhi and Ms Julia Gillard. In the UK, currently both positions—Head of State and Head of Government, are occupied by women. The current British Minister, Ms Theresa May, and the German Chancellor, Angela Merkel, are fine examples of strong leadership.

In 2017, currently[25] there are 20 women holding the office of the Head of State or Head of Government, representing 6.3% of 315 world leaders. In 2016, 22 women occupied the highest political positions in their countries. Currently, there are 13 women that are the highest representatives of their countries, representing 7.3% of the total number of 178 Heads of State in the world. Traditionally, more than the half of them represent the European countries.

It seems, while the rest of the world is embracing the gender parity and women are increasingly leading their countries, some people in India are still living in the dark ages. Proactive, result-oriented, education is the need of the hour.

A Middle Life

Living a *middle life* is a general way of life. The father of a friend visiting from India recently disclosed that he has been writing a book for the last ten years, titled, *Beech Wali Zindagi*, which means *The middle life*. On probing, he said it means most people in India pray to God, and follow a life full of superstitions, due to the fear for God. He said not many people love God. He cited the example of his son and son-in-law, both of whom love to eat meat, but due to their family traditions (rather superstitions) they can't eat meat on Tuesdays, Thursdays or

[25] https://firstladies.international/2017/03/07/2017-women-and-political-leadership-female-heads-of-state-and-heads-of-government/

Mondays. Reportedly, he has advised both of them to either consume meat on all days of the week or totally give it up, but not to struggle in-between. Love God and not fear God.

General Characteristics

One may argue that all above points are symptoms of a middle class which is still climbing on the ascending curve of prosperity.

One can ask, "What is money for?" A person like me could answer, "It is meant for meeting the costs of the essentials of life—food, clothing and shelter, as well as medical assistance when a need arises; education of the children, transportation, some entertainment and holidays. Well, in India, many people may agree with me. However, they will not say what I am going to write here. They also use it for creating and sustaining social divisions, class, status, and to show off they are superior to *others*.

The *other person* is usually none other than one's own brother or sister or a friend or a close relative or a neighbour. The most popular expressions are:

- "*Hum dikhayennge duniya ko ki hum kisi se kum nahin*," meaning "we'll show to the world that we are no less than anyone."
- "*Kya yaad karenghe sub log ki hum ne apne bachon ki shaadi kaise dhoom dhaam se ki*," meaning "People will remember the pomp and show with which we have celebrated the wedding of our children."
- "*Mujhe usey dikhana hai ki hum us sey budh chudh kar kaam kar sakte hain*," meaning, "I have to show to him that I can do things better than him."

Ironically, the other people are the very same people whom they expect to assist and support them in their times of need, e.g. at times of death or sickness or financial distress in the family. But, they don't remember those times of need. They just want the other people to be jealous of them.

What does this all mean? It means the social relationship between people is not very sincere or genuine as it appears to be on the surface. Otherwise, why would anyone with a sound mind try to show off and feed the jealousy experienced by others? In general, Indians are obsessed with showing their own people down.

Sadly, many Indians carry the same psyche and mentality to wherever they go after leaving India. Same showing off, albeit with meagre resources and a hollow foundation, typically characterises them. Many people living outside India generally talk in a manner and glorify themselves as if their forefathers in India were landlords or princes in the past.

Indians must find a reason to divide themselves over region, ethnicity, religion, caste, class etc., a tendency which itself is a white-anting act as it does not allow the community to bond and work together. It potentially creates a non-homogenous society, wherein people of one particular social class or status not only compete within themselves, but also proactively try to push the people of other (lower socio-economic) classes to their lower level where they are potentially exposed to exploitation by the people of higher socio-economic class.

During my visits to India, I have come across many friends and relatives saying to me, with great pride, "Now that we have several malls here in India also and all imported products are available—what is the difference between *foreign* and this place?" How can I explain to these people that foreign is not foreign because of malls; it is because of the quality of life that people live there, for example, the quality of air that they breathe and their 24 x 7 access to clean drinking water from the taps, and the electrical supply, not to speak of numerous other facilities.

1.7 HAPPINESS & MONEY

This section presents some factual figures about the actual level of happiness in India, based on a 2016 data, and a research about the relationship between happiness and wealth.

1.7.1 Is India becoming happier?

India is the fastest growing economy in the world, with a current GDP rate of more than 7%. She is already the third largest economy in the world. Undoubtedly, people in India are becoming more and more affluent with each year, although the rate varies significantly with various sections of the country.

The important question is: "Is India also becoming happier as her economy grows?"

The Sustainable Development Solutions Network (SDSN), a United Nations initiative, published the World Happiness Report 2016, which ranked 156 countries according to their happiness levels.

India was ranked at 118th, well below Somalia (76), China (83), Pakistan (92), Iran (105), Palestinian Territories (108) and Bangladesh (110).

Denmark topped the list, followed sequentially by Switzerland, Iceland, Norway, Finland, Canada, Netherlands, New Zealand, Australia and Sweden.

The report noted, "*People are happier living in societies where there is less inequality of happiness.*" It has been found that, over the last decade or so, happiness inequality has increased significantly in some fast developing economies, such as India, which showed significant gaps between various socio-economic groups.

The World Happiness Index surveys people from various countries every year and ranks them in terms of happiness index.

1.7.2 Can Her Military Strength Make Her People Happy?

Militarily, India is one of the most powerful countries in the world. Her army stands at no 3, air-force at no 4 and navy at no 5 in the world ranking. Overall, she ranks at number 4 in the world in terms of her military strength. The top ten militarily strong countries are: the USA, Russia, China, India, France, the UK, Japan, Turkey, Germany and Italy.

None of these countries figure in the world's top ten happiest countries.

1.7.3 Does Love For Money Make People Happy?

On 17 October 2016, Elizabeth Redman[26], wrote an article in *The Australian*, titled, "*An unhealthy love of money leads to poor financial performance.*"

[26] The North American Correspndent for *The Australian,* based in the US.

With 93 per cent of respondents showing an emotional attachment to money, India topped the list. In comparison, the five happiest countries figured in the bottom half of the list, with Canada at 14th, Sweden at 17th, Australia at 18th, Switzerland at 19th and Netherlands at 20th, indicating that people in relatively happier countries are relatively less attached to money.

Elizabeth's study comprised a global survey of 3,600 investors from across 20 countries[27]. Of those, five countries figured in 2016 in the world's top ten happiest countries–Switzerland, Canada, Netherland, Australia and Sweden.

To determine if a respondent could be considered as a lover of money, the researchers sought their agreement or disagreement with the following five statements:

- I want to be rich.
- Money is important.
- Money is a symbol of my success.
- I like to think and talk about money.
- I'm motivated to work hard for money.

The researchers also tested the respondents on the following three behavioural biases:

- Instant gratification
- Greed-based or fear-based motives
- Hyperactive behaviour

Globally, the countries with people having the highest love of money were observed to be the countries which have high poverty levels, with money mostly seen as a status symbol. Elizabeth concluded: '*The countries with the highest love of money were countries with high levels of poverty, where money is most likely to be seen as a status symbol.*'

The researchers attributed the result of the survey to (a) the capitalistic culture and history of the country; and (b) a social divide in

---

[27] India (93%), China (88%), Brazil (76%), Singapore (71%), Mexico (68%), US (65%), Hong Kong (63%), Chile (61%), South Africa (60%), UAW (58%), Japan (55%), Italy (53%), Germany (47%), Canada (47%), France (41%), Britain (38%), Sweden (37%), Australia (34%), Switzerland (33%), Netherlands (31%).

Percentages reflect respondents showing an emotional attachment to money.

the country. In the countries that scored high on the list, the difference in wealth among different classes was quite pronounced.

"*We found through this research, the more that people love money, the more money they lose,*" Suzanne Duncan, global head of research at the Centre for Applied Research, told *The Australian*. "*People who scored high on the love of money scale make worse financial decisions.*" She added, "*The more prosperous the country is on average, the less people consider money to be a symbol of status. They crave it less. And the reverse is true.*"

1.7.4 Does Spending Money On Others Make People Happy?[28]

In 2014, social researches, Elizabeth Dunn[29]and Lara Aknin[30], summarised the findings of their research study[31] (*Prosocial Spending and Happiness, Using Money to Benefit Others Pays off, edited by Michael Norton*[32]) as follows:

"*Although a great deal of research has shown that people with more money are somewhat happier than are people with less money, our research demonstrates that how people spend their money also matters for their happiness. In particular, both correlational and experimental studies have shown that people who spend money on others report more happiness. The benefits of such prosocial spending among adults around the world, and the warm glow of giving can be detected even in toddlers.*

These benefits are most likely to emerge when giving satisfies one or more core human needs (relatedness, competence and autonomy). The rewards of prosocial spending are observable in both the brain and the body and can potentially be harnessed by organizations and governments."

---

28 Research by Flynn F & Holden, PE Professor of Organizational Behaviour at Stanford Graduate School of Business.

29 Department of Psychology, University of British Columbia

30 Department of Psychology, Simon Fraser University

31 Dunn W E, Aknin L B & Norton M I, 2014, *Prosocial Spending and Happiness, Using Money to Benefit Others Pays off*', *Current Directions in Psychological Science*' (a journal of the Association for Psychological Science)

32 Marketing Unit, Harvard Business School

Earlier in 2013, Elizabeth Dunn and Michael Norton, in their book *Happy Money: The Science of Smarter Spending*[33] also suggested that if you think money can't buy happiness, you're not spending it right.

According to them, the most satisfying way of using money is to invest in others, which can range from giving donation for a noble cause or a charity to buying lunch for a friend. They suggested '*the proclivity to derive joy from investing in others may well be just a fundamental component of human nature.*'

The authors concluded that investing in others can make one feel healthier and wealthier. Giving generously to charities, friends, co-workers and your country (through taxes) could possibly be a productive means to increase your well-being and the quality of life in general.

It is time the above messages are conveyed to the people of India who keep chasing money and material things for happiness. In the process, they drive consumerism which, in turn, breeds corruption and environmental degradation. The result: Humans are increasingly unhappy and unhealthy—physically and mentally.

---

[33] Published by Harvard Business school

CHAPTER 2
Summer 2016 - Welcome to India

2.0 AN UNSOLICITED ADVICE

5 July 2016, 8.30 am.
Domestic Terminal, IGIA, Delhi.

Just a couple of hours agó, I had landed from Perth, Australia, and now I was on my way to Srinagar to meet my father who was on his regular six-week summer visit to Srinagar to escape from an extremely hot and humid environment at Jammu, which he finds unbearable. Normally, he lives at Jammu.

"*Brahmin devta, namaskar*[34]! What are you doing in Australia? You should be serving Bharat Mata[35]! By the way, why are flying to Srinagar? Wasn't your community forced out of the valley?" These words, from a flat-bellied and smart one-star security personnel, greeted and startled me when I went through the routine security check at the domestic terminal. Obviously, based on my boarding card and the passport, this guy had identified my religion, caste, my origins and the current place

---

[34] Indian greetings for a learned person of the Brahmin caste.

[35] In Hindi, *Bharat Mata* means 'Mother India.'

of my residence, but perhaps he wasn't very sure about the intended purpose of my visit to the strife-torn valley.

After having been completed taken aback at this unexpected, rather unprofessional greeting from a security personnel on duty and in uniform, I replied, rather sheepishly, "I am serving Bharat Mata. I have just completed the first draft of my book about my exodus from Kashmir." Upon hearing this, he again surprised me when he asked, "Where is the book? Can I see it please?" Perhaps he was simply trying to do his job and making sure that I was who I was claiming to be. Luckily, on this trip I had carried the hard copy of the first draft copy of the book (*Twenty Two Years*) in my hand bag, for my self-review. I said, "Yes, why not? It is in my hand bag. I can show it to you now if you like." He looked keen and waited for me to unzip my bag and get it out. He quickly flipped a few pages of the book and returned it to me, with a big smile on his face. To my relief, his parting words were, "Thank you, Sir! It was a pleasure meeting with you."

With some relief, I quickly walked towards the boarding gate, with my heart still pounding fast due to anxiety that I had unexpectedly suffered during a routine security check. Upon reaching the boarding gate, I could not stop thinking about my unwanted experience. What could have been the reason that the security personnel, in his early thirties, took so much interest in me?

Did he just pity me because my community was driven out of our homeland or did he just make fun of me for having been driven out from Kashmir? Or, did he feel sorry for me that I had to leave India as a result and, therefore, was he trying to convey to me that India had enough space to accommodate me? Was he trying to remind me about my duties towards India? Who was he? I wondered what he knew about 1990; and how old would he have been at that time? Regretfully, I had not noted the name on his badge; I never do that normally, but now I realised that I should have done so, not for reporting his rather unprofessional behaviour to his superiors but for the sake of my own interest. Without being absolutely sure about his intentions and informal greetings in any case, I would not have reported him and jeopardised his job. Maybe he was just being silly, or smarting off. The whole experience alarmed me and left a bad taste in my memory.

It was an unusual morning; actually very unusual the way it started.

2.1 A MEMORABLE AND UNUSUAL BREAKFAST

Earlier in the morning, at about 7 am, I was received by Subash, a friend and a fellow meditator[36], at the domestic terminal of IGIA after landing at the international terminal at about 5.45 am. Subash drove us to a nearby pristine, grassed, traffic island, located within the airport premises, for a quick home-made breakfast. It was a cloudy and relatively cool morning. To my utter surprise, under the very eyes of some security personnel standing on the traffic island, he parked his car, with its emergency lights flashing, in the extreme left lane of a very wide, multi-lane road section leading to the airport. I reminded him that he could not do so and block a traffic lane. He just smiled and assured me that it would be all right as long as we did not sit there for more than half an hour at the most. Thereafter, he walked to those security personnel and spoke with them.

After seemingly receiving their conditional verbal approval for parking his car, to my extreme surprise, he brought out a beautiful rug and a large picnic basket from the boot of his car. Surprises galore! After laying the rug on the grassed turf, he placed a beautiful plastic picnic sheet on the rug, over which he placed two dinner plates, four lidded food bowls, a thermos flask containing hot water, a pot of milk, a pack of assorted teabags, and a pack of biscuits. Well, it did not end there. Last of all, came out two hand towels, a bottle of water and a small bottle of hand sanitiser.

After laying this breakfast table, he asked me, '*Maharah*[37], would you like to wash your hands with water or prefer to use a hand-sanitiser?"

"I'll wash my hands, *maharah*", I replied, still feeling highly bemused at what was actually happening. He sensed my thoughts and

---

[36] Transcendental Meditation

[37] Kashmiri – means a revered one, spoken with respect.

began, "You had such a short transit time at Delhi. I did not know if there was any better place near the airport than this one where I could take you for breakfast. I thought this place provided us with a nice and cool environment where we could spend some quality time and have our breakfast; you may notice the traffic is relatively quite low at this time of the day." With a cryptic smile on his face, he continued, "I have also requested the weather god to give us some cloud cover for an hour or so to let us sit here in the open and enjoy our breakfast. And, the weather god has thankfully obliged."

I was speechless, as I found no words to respond to him., I found myself giggling and looking around like a child in disbelief. In my wildest imagination, I would not have expected or conceived such a breakfast setting. Finally, I could not resist any longer and had to acknowledge, "Subash Ji, you are a very special person, as is evident this morning, about how you think and do things. I don't see anyone that I know, including me, who would have thought of this venue for such an early morning breakfast picnic." He smiled, as he started removing the lids from the food bowls, one at a time. He looked so settled and happy, with an effulgent face, which was not very surprising to me, as he is a meditator! The breakfast food comprised three home-made vegetarian dishes in three bowls and paranthas[38] in the fourth bowl. Without asking me, he started filling my plate. His love made me defenceless, as I saw myself picking up a piece of paneer[39] from my plate, with a piece of pranatha, and putting it in my mouth. Over the next 15 minutes, with three paranthas and lots of vegetables and paneer down my gullet, we kept munching and talking quickly. He also flicked quickly through the first draft of my book *Twenty Two Years*. Next, he filled our cups with tea and opened a packet of biscuits on a plate. Time seemed to go past swiftly as we chatted. Around 8 am, we wound up from there and rushed back to the airport.

Within the next 10 minutes, we were back in the front car park of the domestic terminal. After exchanging goodbyes and a warm hug, I rushed towards the entrance of the terminal, where my ticket

---

[38] North Indian flat breads.

[39] Ricotta cheese

and passport were checked by the security personnel. When I turned around to take a last look at the area where Subash had dropped me, I noticed that he was still there, seemingly struggling to open the car door while speaking to some people. I felt very concerned, but I had to resist a strong urge to rush out and help him. As I rushed towards the check-in counter, I kept looking over my shoulder, hoping he would have left, but nothing such happened. After receiving my boarding card, I called him over his phone. He said he was locked out. Apparently, one of us, possibly me, had pressed some button at the time of alighting from the car. Although I did not recall pressing anything, I felt guilty and very apologetic. He did not deserve such harassment and inconvenience for getting locked out at such a busy drop off zone at the airport, especially after taking such immense pains hosting me over a memorable breakfast.

Subash's ordeal[40], after hosting me with such exemplary warmth, left a bitter taste in me on that morning, which was otherwise so beautiful.

Rewards don't always follow logic; there are times when noble people are, undeservedly, subject to immense inconvenience or receive punishment for absolutely no apparent reasons. One must always be mindful at every moment in life; for example, in this instance, even while alighting from a car.

A quick reflection on the quality of the breakfast, and the unusual venue where it was eaten, will reveal a lot about how things can happen in India. How many people would go to such an extent, as Subash did, to choose such a venue for the breakfast? It was most unexpected as far as I am concerned. How was it possible? It was Subash's love and care, and his thinking out of the box, howsoever bizarre and unusual that may be. Only an Indian can think and do like that. With my sane mind, I could not have turned down Subash's hospitality—no one could have.

---

[40] Reportedly, Subash engaged a taxi from (and back to) the airport to get a spare car key from his house, which is located about an hour's drive from the airport. Finally, he reached his office around 12.30 pm, thus losing half of the working day.

When some politically motivated people unnecessarily criticise Mr Modi for wearing expensive clothing, which has been gifted to him by his followers, one can only derive that such critics are playing silly games. It will not take much time to deduce that Mr Modi is a very simple person, without much to show off in terms of materialistic wealth or any desire to create a family empire. Such critics are selfish, but their criticism potentially misleads many people and also creates an unnecessary distraction for the government. The country does not need such distractions; people have voted for the government to work. Those who try to disrupt the working of an elected government cause a significant damage to the country. An elected government must be respected by one and all, including the Opposition, and given due time and opportunity for maintaining an undivided focus and on addressing the people's issues and the country's progress.

2.2 NATIONALISM – REALLY?

On reaching the boarding gate, with adrenalin flowing through me, I noticed that most of the passengers had already boarded the plane. For a change, I found I did not have to stand in the queue. I walked briskly through the security gate and boarded a waiting bus which took me to the plane.

After getting seated on the plane, my mind went back to the greetings from that security personnel, "*Brahmin devta, namakar*". These words deeply irked me, just like some undigested food which wants to be thrown out. Having lived in Australia for last couple of decades, I did not feel comfortable with all three words of the greeting: *Brahmin, devta* and *namakar*.

Which part of me was a Brahmin? Just being born in a so-called *Brahmin* family does not make me a Brahmin in a strict sense. I am a professional, and not a Brahmin who would traditionally perform religious rituals or serve as a King's advisor or teach his pupils. Although shades of all these tasks do feature in my daily chores, I also get involved in the business negotiations and in selling my technical skills to my clients, as a trader. Most importantly, I also clean my toilet bowl every day, as well as the inside and outside of the house on a weekly basis.

Which part of me is a *devta*[41]? I am not any God's deputy. I get paid to do my professional work. I don't do any great charity work. Any other tasks that I perform without getting paid are simply born out of my duty as a human towards my fellow beings who share this planet with me.

Namaskar is a general greeting in India, but which the people belonging to the Hindu community usually use while greeting one another. Other communities have their own greetings. I would not expect any greetings, based on any religious background, coming from a security person who must conform to a strict professional conduct and deportment. However, I must remember that, in Indonesia, where Islam is the dominant religion, a hand-folded *namaskar* is the formal greeting of the state.

Also, why was he not happy that I was flying to Kashmir? Was Kashmir off limits to Kashmiri Pandits? Did he forget the number of times that the country's Prime Minister himself visited Kashmir—be it for bonding with the local people, or for raising the morale of the jawans fighting insurgency, or for overseeing relief works after that gigantic flood in the valley a couple of years ago.

With these thoughts, I closed my eyes. The plane sprinted on the runway, making enough noise, which doused my niggling thoughts and flushed them out of my head. I felt relatively peaceful as the plane took off. Once again, I looked forward to meeting my father and my aunt's family in Srinagar. But, after some minutes, my mind suddenly came back to the incident. Why were people trying to undermine the efforts of the Prime Minister, Mr Modi? On the surface, I could have concluded that the security person would have been a nationalist Hindu raising some question: When did Mr Modi ask the NRIs and the people of Indian origins living overseas to return to India and serve the country? He never did! He openly recognises and appreciates the efforts and contributions made by the overseas Indians, wherever they live on the planet, towards their motherland and their new country of residence. All such Indians, through their work, practically serve as brand ambassadors of India and, in the process, through their own

---

[41] God's deputy—a noble and virtuous person.

subtle efforts and ways, bring the rest of the world closer to India. Also, one must never underestimate the significant investments that overseas Indians make in India–through both cash and kind.

In 2017, India and the Indians are well respected in the world, thanks to the millions of overseas Indians and India's hard-working, dedicated, charismatic Prime minister. People are simply drawn towards him, for what he is and what he stands for. He is charismatic and that too for the right reasons. How sad it is to see some people in India criticising him for making frequent foreign visits. The Prime Minister must travel around frequently to meet and discuss common issues with the other world leaders. I call it *political socialisation*. The Indian Prime Minister is a democratically elected leader of India. When he goes overseas, he meets similar democratically elected leaders and representatives of the host countries. In 2017, India can't afford to live in seclusion. Socialisation is extremely important for bonding people, and involves sharing and caring for one another. That only happens when people meet in person and discuss issues face to face at regular intervals, followed by frequent telephone discussions. Politicians are also human beings and they must also connect with politicians of other countries for achieving mutual goals and addressing common issues.

Mr Modi stands for all Indians, irrespective of their region, religion and caste. When did he say that India is a nation only for Hindus? His popular slogan is: "*Sub ka saath, sub ka vikas*", which I interpret as "all people march together for achieving progress and prosperity for all". India belongs to all Indians who live and thrive there.

A smooth landing at Srinagar airport marked my homecoming. I was received by my father and Bashir Bhai, my uncle's chauffeur. The weather was warm and humid, which is usual in the month of July. Enroute to my aunt's home, my thoughts drifted numerous times between my past life in Srinagar and the present time. Things did not look the same. At times, I took a deep breath and prayed for the well-being of all Kashmiri people—Pandits and Muslims. At times, I had a tear or two at the corner of my eyes.

"Life goes forwards; one must remain optimistic", I advised myself.

On my first night in Srinagar, on 5 July 2016, the valley was hit by a massive storm, which caused widespread damage to numerous trees and structures. I visited the Mata Kheer Bhawani Shrine the next day accompanied by my father and aunt. We spent almost the whole day there. It was my son's birthday. Ram ji Halwai cooked traditional yellow rice and vegetarian dishes for us.

In the evening, after some confusion created by the local religious leaders, Eid-ul-Fitr was declared to be celebrated on the next day. On the morning of 7 July 2016, we went to Jaeshta Devi temple, located on the slopes of Zabarwan, off Dal Lake. On the evening of 8 July 2016, the fourth day of my visit, the news of killing of a young militant leader by the security forces spread like wildfire and brewed tension in the air.

On 9 July 2016, I witnessed repeated invasion of a nearby CRPF camp over the course of the day by several mobs of stone-pelting youth (generally 10 to 25 year olds), who shouted vicious verbal abuse at the security forces, provoking and challenging them to come out of their camp. The CRPF jawans exercised utmost restraint and no one was injured on that day. It seemed the youth were acting outside the control of their families. A Muslim lady from across the road came out of her house and yelled at them to go back to their homes. However, within seconds, they broke all her glass window panes. A person shouted, she is a *mukhbir* (means 'an informer'). It was an extremely tense day. I had never before witnessed such unruly mobs and disturbing sights in person in my life. Normally, one sees such scenes on the television from places like Lebanon and Palestine.

I left the valley as per my original scheduled flight (at 3.45 pm) on 10 July 2016. However, that was possible only when I was able to reach the airport by 8 am on that morning, thanks to Bashir Bhai, who took the initiative and dropped me off at the airport while risking his own life. On the way to the airport, I observed the carnage left on the roads by the protesters the day before. When I reached the airport, hundreds of travellers had camped in the open grounds of the airport premises. It appeared to be like a warlike situation. Reportedly, most of the tourists and pilgrims had been camping there since about 3 am that morning. In the airport lounge, many travellers were heard swearing that they would never return to Kashmir. Many visitors reported that their hotels were invaded by angry mobs around 10 to 11 pm on the night before; many had feared for their lives.

Aboard the plane, my fellow passengers were a couple from Bangalore, in their mid-fifties, who were returning home. They had just arrived in Srinagar only a day before for undertaking a pilgrimage to the holy Amarnath Shrine. However, on sensing trouble, they had aborted their plans for the pilgrimage and instead decided to leave the valley immediately, out of fear for their personal safety. Being an original son of the soil, I felt quite embarrassed to hear about their ordeal and the appalling situation that had been created by my fellow Kashmiri brethren in the valley. Out of my sense of ownership of the valley and my responsibility as a host, I apologised to them sincerely for their aborted pilgrimage, utter discomfort and their financial loss. My pride as a hospitable Kashmiri had just melted and flown down a gutter. I felt very small and shameful. My guests were returning home, without a meal in Kashmir. Who would believe such a thing had happened, as Kashmiris were traditionally known to be very warm and hospitable? A very painful realisation hit me, for it seemed Kashmir was finally lost to all—those who were forced to leave the valley a quarter of a decade ago and those who were left behind, irrespective of their religious or geographical divide. Most Kashmiris seemed to be poor victims of a nefarious game-plan, woven around an alien ideology, developed for and driven by a minor section of the Kashmiri community, by foreigners, something never seen before in the valley.

What I had experienced recently in Kashmir (5 to 10 July 2016) shocked me to the core, yet again! Unfortunately, Kashmir seems to have well and truly become embroiled now in a Catch 22 situation! What I saw in Kashmir does not make any sense, whatsoever, to any rational and peace-loving mind.

I had watched in absolute shock, disbelief and bewilderment how young children, as young as 10 years old, attacked the security forces in the aftermath of a young militant leader's death. Interestingly, when the 'educated' father of the slain militant was interviewed about six months before his death, he seemed to have been mentally prepared to see him killed in the name of religion. It is a pity and extremely unfortunate and painful to witness what these young Kashmiri children and youth are doing, or are being coerced, incited, motivated, inspired and encouraged to do, in stark contrast to what their Pandit cousins have been doing outside the valley since 1990.

The Kashmiri children and the youth seem to compromise and endanger not only their future but also their young lives, whereas their Pandit cousins seem to focus, as always, on their education and, thereafter, coexist peacefully with the world community. At the time I saw these children throwing stones on the security personnel, they should have normally been busy elsewhere—at home, or at school or in a playing ground. While the Kashmiri children and youth are seemingly being raised with hate, anger and violence, their counterparts outside Kashmir are being raised as peaceful world citizens. A number of simple questions have been haunting me since my return from Kashmir:

- Did the stone-pelting children really know what they were doing and why? Were these children really under the control of their parents or under the (remote) control of some people whom they may have never met? On whose behest did they act?
- Why do some elders and leaders of Kashmir instigate their children and youth to raid the camps of the security forces and attack them with stones and sticks? Who does not know that it is sheer madness, rather suicidal, to try and snatch the weapons of the security personnel? Therefore, why do these elders and leaders instigate their children and the youth to commit suicide? Why don't these leaders and elders carry out such mad acts themselves?
- Is it a religious war rather than a political issue? If yes, what is the basis of the *religious war*? Who is infringing on the religious freedom of the Kashmiris, now that the Pandits have more or less disappeared?

The so-called political leaders have been crying for *azaadi* (freedom) but do they actually know the meaning of the word? Seemingly not! They must ask the Pandits what real *azaadi* means, as the Pandits may have tasted it after their exodus from Kashmir in 1990.

It is abhorrent to get youth and children injured and killed. History will, perhaps, never forgive the real culprits after they are identified by the majority Muslim community. The current Kashmiri leaders and elders bear the ultimate responsibility for compromising the lives and the future of their younger generations. History may never forgive them!

CHAPTER 3
Autumn 2016
A Newfound Nationalism

3.0 WELCOME TO MUMBAI

21st October 2016, 10.45 am.

Chhatrapati Shivaji International Airport (Terminal 2), Mumbai

I had just arrived from Perth, via Singapore, to attend the wedding ceremony of my cousin at Jammu, scheduled on 24th October 2016. Normally, I should have landed at Delhi, but on this occasion I had decided to first catch up with my friend, Rakesh Misri, at Mumbai and get a feedback from him on my book *My life does not have to be unhappy* that I had been writing at that time.

On the Indian Immigration (Arrival) form, I had scribbled my address in India as my father's home address in Jammu. The Immigration official, a smart looking young man, welcomed me with a warm and genuine smile, but on noticing my Jammu address on the immigration form, he became a little curious about the reasons of my arrival at Mumbai, instead of Delhi. I explained to him that I had a confirmed air ticket, dated 23rd October 2016, to fly to Jammu, where my father lived, but before flying to Jammu I had wished to catch up with my best friend, who lived and worked at Mumbai. I also offered to provide him with the contact details of my friend just in case he wanted to verify my claim. However, he thanked me with a warm smile and politely declined my offer. After completing the formalities, he wished me a nice stay in Mumbai. I genuinely thanked him. Deep inside, I was very impressed with his through professionalism, coupled with his warmth and politeness, as the host country's first representative at the immigration.

Immigration counters virtually mark a country's border at an international airport; therefore, when a person walks past an immigration checkpoint, one walks into the host country. The Immigration officials are actually the first representatives of the host country and their friendly behaviour is paramount for leaving a lasting impression on the mind of a visitor, especially a foreign national, who has just arrived in the country, especially if the visitor is arriving for the first time.

My Singapore Airlines flight had landed about 15 minutes before its scheduled time of 10.30 am and, because I did not carry any checked-in luggage, I found myself in a position to leave the terminal building well before 10.45 am. That meant I had a wait of at least 15 minutes outside the terminal building, in the Mumbai warm and humid environment, before meeting Gajanan Patel, my friend's chauffeur, who was expected to receive me at 11 am and take me home.

To minimise my exposure to the warm and humid air outside, I used those precious 15 minutes to freshen myself at the airport facilities, in an air-conditioned environment. I also connected with the free Wi-Fi at the airport and sent some messages around the world to inform my family in Perth, my dad at Jammu, as well as Rakesh in Mumbai, about my safe landing at Mumbai. Importantly, I also bought some Indian currency at the airport Thomas Cook booth for meeting my daily expenses in India.

In India, for personal and internet safety reasons, I prefer not to use my credit cards or my Australian bank card at local ATM booths, although many Australians have reported no issues with using their credit and bank cards in India. Therefore, every time I visit India, I must buy enough Indian currency, which can last me comfortably through my visit. Usually, I exchange the currency at the airport itself.

At 11 sharp, as soon as I stepped outside the terminal building, the warm, humid air hit me. It is uncomfortable for a newly arrived traveller, especially if that person has arrived from a place with a relatively moderate climate and then lived in an air-conditioned environment (in the plane) for over 14 hours prior to stepping out of the terminal building. Furthermore, the air quality in India presents its own challenge. With warm and humid air filling my lungs, I suddenly felt a little drained, as my body started sweating and recovering from that initial shock. Of course, it does not take more than a few hours or so to get acclimatised.

Ganjanan Patel, aged about 60 or so, had driven me around during my previous Mumbai visits. I stated searching for his face amongst a large crowd of waiting people. Soon I spotted him with a placard bearing my name. As I noticed him, he waved towards me, and I waved back excitedly. Hurriedly, I walked towards him and, after exchanging initial greetings and pleasantries, we rushed towards the car park. However, upon reaching there, he could not find his car. It took him more than 15 minutes to locate the car; he did not remember the car park level where he had parked it. So, that completed my quick acclimatisation with the Mumbai climate. I felt a little more tired and sweaty by the time the car was found. He apologised sincerely a number of times for the inconvenience caused due to his lack of mindfulness while I tried to reassure him not to worry too much, as such things can happen with anyone and actually have happened with me as well in the past.

In the car, we touch based about our families and discussed the general life in Mumbai and India as a whole.

We also discussed the current situation at the Indo-Pak border and the probability of a full scale war breaking out between the two countries. At the time of booking my air tickets for this trip, I was aware and mentally prepared about the possibility of the breakout of a full war[42]. Prior to my departure from Perth, I had apprised my family about any such eventuality and also made the necessary arrangements just in case I was caught in a war. My father's home at Jammu is just about 15 km from the Indio-Pak border, as the crow flies, and things can happen quickly.

As they say, good times pass very fast, especially when one catches up with one's best friend and if that friend has also been a college mate. The next day and a half went quickly like a breeze.

An evening walk on the Marine Drive at the time of sunset is always a joy and an experience to remember. The sea breeze that blows across your face as you walk along the footpath is so refreshing. At that time, on any day of the week, the parapet along the seawall along the entire length of Marine drive seats thousands of people who look cheerful and relaxed after their work day. People in Mumbai invariably

---

42 Since my previous visit to Srinagar in July 2016, widespread protests, mainly by stone-pelting children and youth, had taken place in the Kashmir valley on a daily basis against the Indian government after the killing of Burhan Wani, a Hizbul Mujahedeen militant, by the Indian forces, on 8 July 2016. Reportedly, more than 80 civilians have died in the protests and more than 1,000 people have been injured, including more than 3,000 security forces injured since then.

On 18 September 2016, four militants attacked an army base at Uri, in Kashmir, and killed 19 Indian Army soldiers. India accused Pakistan based Islamic militant organisation, Jaish-e-Muhammad, for the attack. The following day, the Indian Army said that it reserved the right to respond "at the time and place of our own choosing." Eleven days after the Uri attack, on 29 September 2016, following considerable pressure from the Indian public, the Indian Army suddenly announced that it had conducted "surgical strikes" against suspected militants in Pakistani-administered Kashmir and inflicted "significant casualties" on the militants. Indian media reported the casualty figures in the range of 35 to 50, which Pakistan has continued to reject vehemently, stating that Indian troops had never crossed the Line of Control (LOC) but did admit that skirmishes had taken place at the border in which two Pakistani soldiers had been killed and nine wounded.

In the following days, India and Pakistan continued to exchange heavy gun fire and shelling along the LOC, in the Kashmir region, and the international border in the Jammu region, resulting in the temporary dislocation of thousands of people and some civilian deaths on the Indian side, in addition to destruction of some civilian homes, properties and loss of cattle.

come across as disciplined, cheerful, fun loving, peaceful and friendly. Perhaps, it is that traditional Mumbai (erstwhile Bombay) culture that is so addictive that all immigrants into Mumbai just imbibe it seamlessly.

My personal experience with Mumbai is that, in general, people are relatively straightforward, honest and friendly. One can trust a taxi driver or any pedestrian for receiving directions to go to a place one is looking for.

3.1 TRAFFIC JAMS AND ROAD HAZARDS

After a two-day stay at Mumbai, I landed at Jammu on the afternoon of 23rd October 2016. Jammu looked as usual, with construction work for a new flyover along the main arterial road to the airport going on. Traffic on the roads, both motorised and pedestrian, seemed to be denser than the last time I visited the City of Temples.

The traffic density on my usual routes of movement at Jammu, such as TalabTillo, Bohri Road and the Akhnoor Road, seemed to have crossed my already higher limits of tolerance. The reasons are: more vehicles hitting the streets every day, and man-made traffic jams caused primarily due to a total lack of knowledge about standard, common-sense, traffic rules by the motorists. Any vehicle can stop anywhere, even at the crossings, and create bottlenecks.

Private mini buses, which provide the bulk of the public transport, are seemingly the main culprits for endless traffic woes, which become unbearable in the peak rush hours of the day. It can be a traumatic experience if one is caught in a traffic jam especially when one is rushing to catch a train or a plane. The traffic issues are such that one must allow at least two to three hours of travel to cover a distance of about 10 km and reach the Jammu Railway station or Jammu Airport. During the wedding season, one must allow an additional travel time of at least an hour to cover the same distance. About three years ago, one of my relatives missed his train after he was caught up in a traffic jam caused by a wedding procession, for nearly three hours. Ironically, he had precautionarily allowed about three hours to reach the railway station, which is only 9 km from his home. It is not hard to imagine the dire consequences of getting caught in one of those traffic jams in case of a medical emergency when you are rushing a patient to a hospital. How can ambulances really move?

As for the safety, the private mini buses not only cause severe bottlenecks, by dropping and picking up passengers from anywhere, even standing in the middle of a road, that is hardly two lanes wide, but also create serious hazards for pedestrians, smaller two-wheeled and other light vehicles. Mini buses compete with one another in picking passengers from the roadside. During this trip, I heard that a 24-year-old youth, riding a motorcycle, was knocked down by an overtaking minibus and killed on the spot.

I am not very sure if motor driving licenses are issued by the relevant government department after conducting proper, international standard, theory and practical driving tests.

There is an interesting anecdote that I would like share in this book. One night, a friend of mine at Jammu was returning home when he was stopped on a turn by a friendly looking traffic policeman. When he rolled down his window, the policeman asked him if he could get a lift up to a certain point, which was incidentally on my friend's way home. My friend obliged and the policemen sat on the front passenger seat of the car. On the way, they started chatting about general life issues. Suddenly, my friend used the dipper to lower the car headlight beam to allow an oncoming car to cross safely. When the policeman saw this, he asked my friend how he had done it? My friend was surprised and showed him how he had lowered the car headlight beam. The policeman exclaimed with surprise, "*achha, aisa bhi hota hai?*" ("*Oh, it can be like this also*?"). In the olden days, the upper half of the headlight would be painted black to keep the headlight beam on the lower side. When my friend heard this, he was utterly surprised and confused at the policeman's ignorance. He abruptly stopped the car and politely asked the policeman to get down. And the policeman complied. Later, when I heard this story, I asked my friend, "Why did you ask the policeman to get off your car in the middle of nowhere? Shouldn't you have dropped him on humanitarian grounds at his designated point?" My friend replied, "No, that policeman did not deserve to wear his uniform. How can one be a traffic policeman if one does not know such simple things about a car?"

I agreed, but still thought that my friend should not have abandoned that policeman in the middle of nowhere. Maybe my Australian values would not have allowed me to be the judge, jury and the executioner. That guy would have been returning to his family after a long work day. Yes, I agree he was seemingly ignorant about how things work in a modern car; maybe he did not own a car or perhaps he had never driven one. But the issue was not about his knowledge of modern cars. My friend had originally agreed to give him a lift based on humanitarian grounds, and not based on the policeman's know-how about cars. So, deep inside, I questioned my friend's value system. Normally, in such situations, human considerations should be allowed to prevail over any personal judgement.

People don't seem to know standard traffic rules; for example, no vehicle should be allowed to stop within a distance of at least 50 m from a road crossing. It is a common experience that road crossings in Jammu cause serious bottlenecks and traffic jams that sometimes last for hours together. Vehicles must not be allowed to stop anywhere they want.

There must be designated spots where a public vehicle can stop and there must be stretches on every road where no vehicle is allowed to stop at all.

How about wearing seat belts? Generally, people don't care about their safety. A common explanation that I have been hearing is, "Oh, don't worry, it is only a short distance and the traffic is moving so slowly. So, no need to wear a seat belt!"I am sick and tired of hearing this explanation and then educating the person that, even when you drive at a speed of 10 km per hour, sudden application of full brakes can potentially unsettle the driver and cause a serious injury. Not many people have been convinced though.

3.2 ONE TO ONE PERSONAL INTERACTIONS

This section presents a few interesting vignettes of my trip to Jammu, and provide a broad cross-section of the mindset that people have at Jammu. I have felt a pained and concerned about the shallow and lopsided views that some educated people hold about some common social, national and environmental issues. Obviously, they may not be thinking deep enough, but how can educated people show such ignorance?

On the brighter side, the country seems to be populated with all kinds of people, some very bright, progressive and alive to the real issues and some totally ignorant. As long as the former outnumber the latter, the country will keep surging ahead towards a brighter and better tomorrow. Concern remains if the opposite is the case in reality.

3.2.1 Symbolic Vegetarianism

My cousin's wedding function comprised a number of dinners and lunches at a popular wedding resort at Jammu. The following chats happened on the day of the last lunch, two days after the wedding, which the bride's family hosted exclusively for the groom's family and their closest relatives. In Kashmir, the function is called *gara-achhun*, which means '*welcome to our home*'. Personally, I did not understand any need for this additional feast, given that, just two days ago, on the wedding day, we had been received by the bride's family and fed a lavish dinner.

As we were all seated in a hall being served with both vegetarian and non-vegetarian entrée and a range of soft drinks, I decided to ask the bride's father directly about the reason why he hosted this additional feast. I just could not hold back—perhaps my Aussie stripes were pushing me to do so. So, I walked to the front of the hall and stepped on the dais where the bride's father was standing. On seeing me walk towards him, he gave me a welcoming smile and held his hand forward to shake mine. I introduced myself once again, assuming he may not remember me from our last introduction when he must have received hundreds of guests like me. But he did seem to remember me. After congratulating him for successfully performing the wedding ceremony of his daughter and thanking him for his invitation to this special lunch, I asked him, "Sir, if you don't mind, could you please advise me why you had to host this additional lunch for so many people, considering you had just hosted all of us, and many more, on the wedding night, just two days ago?"

He was a little surprised to hear this. He replied, "Sir, that was a general reception dinner, but today's lunch is special. It is exclusively for the groom's family and his closest relatives."

I continued, "Sir, you could have combined this ceremony with the earlier wedding dinner function, couldn't you?"

He replied, "On that day, you people were served a vegetarian dinner. But today's lunch is special with meat based preparations."

I thanked him and walked back to my seat. Later, I had a discussion with my father and a few other people about the validity of this lunch. I was not very happy with the reasoning that meat makes a feast special.

My question to everybody was, "Of all the people, why are Kashmiri Pandits so fond of meat and why do they consider vegetarian feasts as ordinary?"

To this, one of the gentlemen, visibly irritated by my question, replied sarcastically, "What is your problem? If that guy has the money to host this lunch, let him spend it. Just enjoy. And, if nobody eats meat, what will happen to our environment? We will see sheep and goats flocking everywhere."

I was shocked to hear this answer, especially considering the gentleman has reportedly a Bachelor's degree in the agricultural sciences.

I shook my head in disbelief and firmly replied, "Sir, it is a well-established fact that cattle emission is one of the major sources of the greenhouse effect. Plus, from an environmental point of view, meat eating is not sustainable, as water resources keep on dwindling. Do you know that it takes about 10,000 litres of water to produce one kilogram of meat; 1,000 litres of water to grow one kilogram of rice and just one litre to grow one kilogram of potatoes? I am disappointed with my community that meat eating is given such importance, and that too without any regard for ethical, animal rights and environmental considerations."

On hearing this, the gentlemen got angry and admonished me, "You must never criticise your own community. You may criticise others but not your own people, whatever be the case."

I walked off silently. There was absolutely no point in continuing any further discussion with this gentleman. While the rest of the developed and western world is moving steadily towards vegetarianism and veganism, especially the young adults, for a range of reasons, which include empathy for animals and animal rights, and the medically proven health benefits for humans, this gentleman seemed to be still entrenched in the previous century.

Based on my personal observations, the percentage of meat-eaters could actually be growing in India. I have come across many Indian youth who relish eating meat but come from traditional vegetarian families; some of them actually seem to be obsessed with meat eating, like drug addiction. A couple of reasons could be: the general poverty in the past when only the rich afforded meat and the growing affluence in certain sections of the community as a result of the growing economy of the country.

Not many people know that animals too have rights and a day in the year—3rd October) is celebrated as the World Animal Day.

As per Wikipedia[43]:

- Australia is the leading western country in the world with an increasing vegetarian population (about 11.2%), followed by Italy (about 10%).
- India is reported to have the world's largest vegetarian population (about 40%).
- In 2016, a Roy Morgan Research reported, "Between 2012 and 2016, the number of Australian adults whose diet is all or almost all vegetarian has risen from 1.7 million people (or 9.7% of the population) to almost 2.1 million (11.2%)".
- In 2000, a Newspoll survey (commissioned by Sanitarium) reported 44% of Australians ate at least one meat-free evening meal a week, while 18% said they prefer plant-based meals.
- Animal rights organisations in Australia, such as Animal Liberation, promote vegan and vegetarian diets. "Vegetarian Week" runs from 1st to 7th October every year.

Humans have a duty to care for other living beings on the planet. Our survival and sustainability on the planet depends as much on all other living beings as their survival is dependent on us. We must

---

43 https://en.wikipedia.org/wiki/Vegetarianism_by_country

move from an outdated caveman mentality that animals are meant only for human consumption. Animals are there to render a balance to our eco-system. Therefore, with open minds and an educated outlook, we must change. We must, therefore, make a proper use of our intelligence in our dietary habits. We are no longer living the lives of hunters and gatherers or cave dwellers. On the contrary, we are increasingly becoming less and less active physically. We need to eat more plant based foods.

3.2.2 Hollow Nationalism

A friend visited me at my father's home at Jammu. Over tea, as usual, we discussed a range of topics, which included the local, national and international politics, common social issues and sports.

Somehow, as had happened numerous times in the past also, we started having a strong difference of opinion about a number of things. When he could not convince me with his arguments, identifying me as a foreigner, he said, "What are you saying? Our country is booming. People are becoming richer. Indian youth are spreading all over the world; you can't stop them. You guys are fed with wrong information about India by foreign writers and journalists, who always have a hidden agenda to discredit India and her history. Who are your Wordsworth and Shakespeare? Our Kalidasa was much better than them. You must read books on India by Indian scholars and historians, and not only by the foreign writers."

I replied, "My issue is not with all those numerous areas where India has made progress since her independence. Like you, I am also a son of the soil and I very proud of those outstanding achievements. I am, however, deeply worried about the basic essentials of life in India, such as clean air and clean drinking water, less traffic and pollution on the roads, a clean India and not something you see at the entrance of our street, with piles of junk and rubbish on one side, or that overflowing drain in the street with toxic and stagnant water, breeding insects and other nasty organisms.

By the way, have you read any of Kalidasa's books? If yes, in which language? And how about Shakespeare and Wordsworth; what do you know about them? Have you read them? For that matter, how many people in the world know about Kalidas? I am not saying Kalidas was not a great writer. He was, but why should we compare him with anyone else? If you really care about Kalidas, why don't you go on a world tour and give speeches everywhere in the world to promote Kalidas."

My friend looked a bit sheepish and did not say anything. We moved on.

3.2.3 Positive Conversations

The following chats took place between Subash, a friend and I in the period between September and November 2016, before and after the Uri militant attack in Kashmir.

3.2.3.1 A spiritual chat

I had seen a dream in which I saw myself in Pakistan occupied Kashmir, in a hilly setting, with tall conifers standing proud all around. In a large clearing, I saw many tall, newly constructed but partly finished blocks of residential buildings. But I did not see many people around. Next evening, I discussed my dream with Subash over the phone, which included the following conversation, in September 2016.

Subash: "Whatever is within our realm, just cherish that.... In case of a dream...let time decide...because we can just pretend to decipher the dream as per our convenience only...that may or may not be a reality."

Bill: "Yes, it may not be the reality. Nothing is. Or everything is!"

Subash: "Yes...it is better to be truthful to yourself...we don't exactly know...so why ponder? Simply relax. Existing in the present is what is important...past or future is not the reality. Dream...is a past now...no need to hold on to it...just live and enjoy the present...this very moment...it greatly helps. Joy accompanies such state always... bliss follows now and then."

Bill: "Long time back, you said, 'every individual's reality and world is different'."

Subash: "Just be…everything is within us....the inner self is the unchanging reality and the relative is ever changing reality..."

Bill: "You are as complete as the whole universe—the *Brahmand*."

Subash: "So are you. Everyone is...the only difference is in the realisation of this very truth....therein comes our role as individuals. Since knowledge is based in consciousness...we just need to meditate to raise the bar and that too in a natural way...not stressfully. Knowledge is what makes us realise the truth...self-knowledge... self-referral knowledge..."

Bill: "Which bar? Which knowledge? It is like chasing a fly...you run after it and it runs away from you. Just stabilise and be where you are and it lands naturally on you. Knowledge is infinite; a finite mind can't fathom the infinite, so just let go. Too much thinking is an impediment to letting go. Religion is anti-spirituality. Our Gods are ever present within and around us and we are unable to visualise them because we are trained to see Gods in the human form and that can be an impediment in seeing the omnipresence of God. Our spirit is not finite; so how can we dissolve ourselves without unlearning all that we have learnt with our finite senses? At some stage, a rocket has to let go of the booster engine to go ahead unhindered.

"People only remember the pictures of Ram and Krishan but not their teachings. We get caught up in images. People kneel before images or idols out of fear, or perhaps reverence, but seemingly not out of love. If we really loved our deities, we don't need to fear them and kneel before them. I never knelt before my mother or *Bhaisahib*, our spiritual master. Why? Because I loved them! We need images to remind us about the higher being. Why? We are unable to transcend the form and shape of our deities or Gurus and, therefore, are unable to connect with them spiritually.

"Wisdom, perhaps intelligence also, is independent of any formal education. Some are naturally born with wisdom and some never get it despite being educated. It is a natural Divine gift. Meditation removes the dirt from Consciousness (the soul), which is the reflection of *Param-atm*a (the Super-consciousness). Once layers of dirt (ego) vanish, one gains the attributes of *Param-atma*. Spirituality can't be taught. It is an individual specific matter.

"There is no need to try and understand the process of spirituality. Just meditate and do as your consciousness says. Meditation is like medication for the mind. Once you take a medicine, you don't need to know how it works; you just take it as per the doctor's advice and then forget about it. Similarly, after you meditate, just forget about it. There is no need to go deep into all its processes.

"Life can't be lived and understood through words spoken by others. My life's learning is: Simplify your thoughts. Be yourself, whosoever you are; the way you are; wherever you are. Find your own purpose and meaning of life. Listen to your consciousness; it will always keep you on the path of *Dharma*(Righteousness). Carry your own torch with you to show you the way. When we switch a light on, a room illuminates; similarly when we are illuminated from within, a whole community and the nation illuminates. The problems with India and the rest of the world are:

Not everyone meditates; may be less than 1% people do. It is very difficult to convince people to learn and practice meditation. All those who learn to meditate don't commit themselves to the practice 100% in accordance with the original instructions from the teacher. They complicate the process. The basic techniques are so simple; just follow them.

Our esteemed Prime Minister, Mr Modi, was instrumental in getting the UN recognise 21st June as the World Yoga Day. What more could he do? He needs people like us to drive his message across the nation.

Don't use much jargon, it puts people off. Let us not quote others. People want to hear what we say and not what our teacher says. Our spirituality must get reflected in our spontaneity and our righteous actions, which must be carried out not only for our own benefit but for the greater good and benefit of all other fellow beings on this planet, without any fear, discrimination or bias."

Subash: "All Meditators are wise souls…that is why they practice TM[44] ... to find peace and joy..."

Bill: "You are a wise soul; I am not. All people are not!"

3.2.3.2 Indian patriotism

The following conversation took place between Subash and I towards the end of September 2016 in the aftermath of the Uri militant attack

---

44 Transcendental Meditation

in Kashmir and India's surgical strike across the Line of Control in response.

Subash: "War is a continuous game...you hit us...we hit you. But we hit our way...at the place and timing of our own choosing. One thing is clear—our PM was at it all the time since the 18th and it is reported he was awake during the time of the strike...till he got the message it was over."

Bill: "I am highly concerned about the perception about the strikes. We must carefully manage the perception of our Kashmiri cousins, that of the real enemy across the border, and the world overseas. Perception is everything in these situations.

India must manage that aspect wisely, carefully through the provision of the consistent details of the strikes carried out and by holding a sustained and consistent position. Consistency is the key, otherwise the credibility is lost. Kudos to India—to the jawans[45] and her political leadership!"

Subash: "The world knows Mr Modi very well. He has never attacked but when India is hit, he will ensure that the guilty are punished. My personal view is that he is a patriot who wants nothing except the safety and prosperity of his nation."

Bill: "Yes, he is the kind of leader who can inspire our *jawans*. India must trust her *jawans* and they will deliver when the country needs them, they have always done so."

Subash: "It was only due to the morale of the forces that the strike was carried out."

(On another terrorist attack in Srinagar)—

Bill: "This is what I was talking about the other day. No consistency. It puts a question mark on everyone's narratives (media, army and government) and their versions of an event. One can't believe everything that is being fed to the Indian public."

Subash: "No country in the world can maintain consistency against self-destructive terrorists at any point of time and that too in a place like Kashmir where they are being sheltered and provided with logistical support. Our current political set up is trying to plug

---

[45] Indian Army soldiers

the loopholes in the security of our armed forces. That is why this attack, though similar to the Uri attack, was foiled although we lost one young BSF jawan who came in the line of direct and unpredictable fire. Pak Army is facing a severe credibility crunch at home, so they are bound to hit us."

Bill: "Never believe anything from anyone without self-verification. Reliance upon one's own *budhi* (wisdom) is essential for attaining the real freedom. Freedom of thought and expression is the real freedom. Don't accept anything blindly without examining it."

3.2.3.3 Mind over matter

The following conversation took place on 15 October 2016 after my daily morning run in Perth, during which I took a picture of an early morning rainbow on the western horizon.

Subash: "Marvellous nature....a perfect rainbow is visible. Great click. VIBGYOR clearly visible if the picture is zoomed."

Bill: "This morning, for a while, I was running into a strong headwind and rain, amazingly with a bright sun shining at my back. Up ahead, two beautiful rainbows (one lighter) glorified a dark cloudy sky. That is what one gets when one runs in the rain (no pain, no gain). I was wet (both rain and sweat) at the end of it, but it is always like that.

My final one km run back home is uphill, when I have already done 6 to 10 km and my legs are tired—it becomes a real battle of mind over body. A strong headwind this morning was agonisingly slowing me down while running uphill, but it also soothed my body and my soul in the process. All evens out."

Subash: "Just keep going...we know how to adjust with everything..."

Bill: "Fight is within us only! There is no bigger enemy outside of us."

Subash: "There is no fight when we are connected with ourselves... it is just smooth always...totally frictionless..."

Bill: "Soldier on, every moment."

Subash: "Yeah...a true soldier...a soldier of God. No killing, no arms or weapons... just love..."

Bill: "I don't belong to any man-made group, community, religion, country etc. I work more or less autonomously at my office. I am loosely tied with my family and friends. I have earned it. The universe exists within me. Or, conversely, you can say, I am everywhere, albeit with limitations. I have no desire to know more than what I already know. Nothing surprises me now. I like to observe simple things in life, childlike. The whole nature is an open book to read, nothing is hidden. Simple contemplation is all that is required."

3.2.3.4 Freedom & Independence

On 23rd October 2016, at mid-day I landed at Jammu after taking off from Mumbai that morning. The following conversation took place on 24th October 2016.

Subash: (Based on a picture of marigold flowers taken at home in Jammu.) "Appears you are at Jammu."

Bill: "At home with my dad… Jammu is still warm… but indoors at home feels comfy."

Subash: "I could get it...the flowers and colour of soil. And it is so pleasant during night and morning also at Jammu…"

The following conversation took place on 29th October 2016.

Subash: "May see tomorrow's dawn at Jammu. I am leaving by Rajdhani tonight."

Bill: "Have a nice day and a safe journey. See you at 5.30 am tomorrow at the Jammu Railway station. You will be dropped later in the morning at the ashram. Just relax."

Subash: "Thank you but please do keep enjoying yourself at your home. I need to move independently as you know. I don't even think of going anywhere except the *ashram*. Doing so keeps me in a different world and, at no cost would I like it to be disturbed. I highly regard your concern."

Bill: "You are fully independent. See you at 5.30 am at the railway station. After that we'll do as you want. Just relax. I am also a guest here for a few more days and then I am gone. It is sheer coincidence and nothing else that we are both in the same city on this planet. Coincidence! I respect your independence as I value mine. We are both free in that space."

Subash: "Always grateful for your understanding attitude. Would prefer to see you at the *ashram* any time during my stay. Since my mobile will not be working at Jammu, I urge you to kindly enjoy your daily routine instead of coming to the railway station. I will not be comfortable if you come. You are always close to my heart. Hope you accept my sincere request and let me move on my own. I do not even bother OP (Subash's elder brother) when I come to the *ashram*.

3.2.3.5 Demonetisation-I

The following conversation took place in the aftermath of a sudden announcement of demonetisation of Rupees 500 and 1000 currency notes by the Government of India on 8th November 2016.

Subash: "Why is RBI issuing Rupee 2,000 notes? Is it designed to eradicate the black money issues, using state of the art indigenous Nano technology? This bold decision has brought shivers in the political class and all black money hoarders. The common people are happy and feeling elated."

Bill: "What about those garlands that are put around the necks of grooms? They look so obscene. Shouldn't the government also ban those garlands, as they disrespect the legal tender?"

Subash: "They will continue to be used as garlands even with the new currency. No need to ban them...let people decide for themselves. Usually, we see that all saner elements of the society never use such things. It pleases only those who take pride in showing off. The impact of the 8thNovember decision will be huge and beyond anyone's imagination."

Bill: "I feel sorry for India's internal and external enemies. They will die of hunger."

Subash: "Fake and counterfeit money is all gone waste now...a big blow to all enemies of the country, including the miscreants in Kashmir who have been thriving on counterfeit and black money...otherwise how could they survive without doing any work for the last four months? A much bigger crisis has engulfed millions in India who have tons of black money. They are really worried and sinking. It is really a master stroke by the PM and this government. Hopefully, we come to know about the real economic health by the end of December 2016.

Interestingly, only Congress, AAP and a few other politicians are complaining. Also, AK is complaining, as must have hoarded tons of black money for elections in Punjab. Congress has been caught napping, with no remedies to save their black money. All big businessmen who used to transact in cash are feeling the tremors."

3.2.3.6 Regional politics

The following out-of-box conversation took place on 10 November 2016 on a very light note. It was a conversation of 'all things considered', nothing serious, purely hypothetical and not intended to offend anyone.

Bill: "A master stroke would be to befriend China. That may provide a permanent solution to the Pak, China and Kashmir issues."

Subash: "But China has its own interests in Pak. But still we have managed to contain China to a great extent."

Bill: "Let India meet China's interest so that China does not need Pak anymore."

Subash: "Pak has a bankrupt army and is a terror state...we are dealing with them with a heavy hand on a regular basis on the borders. We can't allow China to use our nation for its concerns. Once Pak is dealt with effectively...only then will China need India in the areas like Baluchistan etc. So these are big issues and have to be left for time to decide. Otherwise, we have always been friendly with China, but it has time and again backstabbed India. So there is a lot of mistrust. It is not at all possible given China's strategy to surround India and contain it... It is not so simple an equation. China sees us as a competitor in the region."

Bill: "My strategy would be to work closely together with China to tackle nuisance from Pak. Let us revisit the distant past. Historically, the Chinese emperor would help the king of Kashmir against the West Asian invaders. Buddhism binds the two ancient civilisations. Let us use diplomacy."

Subash: "India has revived its relations with all SAARC nations and East Asian Countries...which again is worrying China. But it does not bind the Communist China that has no love for Buddhism. There is a big shift. It needs China to become a democracy first...only then can we find many more friends in China."

Bill: "SAARC is not worth the time spent on it. India will be better off befriending, not confronting China."

Subash: "India has always done that. But China wants to contain India...which India is not ready to accept at any cost. That is the biggest difference. Our PM has to tackle our multi-party democracy on every front while the Chinese government is free of all such concerns. India can't afford dictatorship and China won't allow democracy. A sharp contrast, politically!

"I enjoy Indian democracy every moment. I can't vouch for others. Had it not been so…how could Kashmiri Muslims live so happily? Had it been China, they would have been crushed. Democracies have replaced autocracy and dictatorships...it is an ever changing world. Nothing is permanent here."

Bill: "You have also created many 'demigods' in several parts of India—celebrity politicians, and several of them have detailed succession plans involving their own family members… do you call that democracy? It is like the old days of royalty—kings and princes in waiting to ascend the throne… India likes kings and princes… Indians like to bow to people, especially those who are rich and powerful."

Subash: "So we just welcome whatever comes. It is a worldwide phenomenon. ...no country is excluded…"

Bill: "India will always lag far behind China."

Subash: "That is a fact but that doesn't mean we stop trying to get better and bigger. There is a mixed bag everywhere. In some countries, governments work as goons, while in other nations, goons run the governments—law breakers are seen in every nook and corner of the world."

Bill: "The word democracy comes from the two Greek words—Demos (people) and Kraita (rule). Abraham Lincoln defined it later as 'government of the people, by the people, for the people'. Until 1947, Indians never tasted democracy in the true sense.

3.2.3.7 Living issues in India

The following chat occurred on 12th November 2016.

Bill: "I have still not recovered fully from my sickness that I got in India. It has been about a week since I returned. Most people I met there were sick due to a number of pollution related reasons. I am waiting for surgical strikes from God (as it is beyond any man) on India's main existential threats like pollution, corruption etc.

"The current surgical strike on black and fake money is highly commendable as long as banks do their proper job now and report defaulters and criminals, otherwise it is useless.

"Your view and vision of India may slightly differ from mine. Your perspective is based on a competition with Pakistan and China. My perspective is much more global. I want India's peaceful coexistence with her neighbours and a respectful standing in the world. I am very concerned with the day-to-day living and the general health of the common man in India. Charity alone does not help. Clean air, clean drinking water and fast moving traffic on the roads are the basics for gauging the health of a country. Sadly, not many politicians seem to be bothered about them."

Subash: "India is evolving. Big reforms are taking place. The PM is working towards *Swachh Bharat*...our standing in the international forum is improving. Let's see how people adapt to the changes. There is an effort from the PM to change the mindset of the nation, which will form the basis of the change."

Bill: "It is not about one person who sleeps for under four hours a night; it is about 1.3 billon people, who must take some responsibility for themselves and the people around them. The PM can't do everything all by himself. People must follow him whole heartedly. People must become conscientious and work to make their country liveable and cleaner. They must also take some responsibility upon themselves and do their bit for the country. As John F Kennedy (former American President) once said to the American citizens, '*My fellow Americans, ask not what your country can do for you, ask what you can do for your country*'.

"Hopefully, after this (demonetisation) outstanding success, people should also be able to breathe cleaner air, drink cleaner water, purchase genuine medicines and see lesser traffic jams on the roads. *Ache din zaroor ayenge* (good days will definitely arrive) when that happens. Unfortunately, any open minded person, with reason and analytical capability, can assess where India is heading to at the present."

3.2.3.8 Demonetisation-II

The following conversation took place between 15 and 19 November 2016.

Subash: "These politicians opposing demonetisation should know people's mood."

Bill: "I believe the PM can generate significant support for himself by alleviating the common person's troubles caused due to issues with cash withdrawals at ATMs and banks. A common person on the street will judge the government based on the degree of convenience in withdrawing cash. Therefore, all ATMs and banks must be filled with cash and the ATMs queues shortened. That is the *mantra.*"

Subash: "ATM machines are being recalibrated and the banks are doing things but it still takes time. However, the trouble was created by the 'paid' labourers who caused long queues while exchanging notes for their masters. Now inking of index finger will fix that up so that no one can approach the bank for currency exchange more than once. Also, smaller and new ATM machines are being installed and utilised for easing the withdrawal issues.

"The post offices have been asked to visit hospitals in their areas and distribute currency to the patients. Also, huge amounts of cash was being deposited in 0-balance, Jan Dhan accounts of ordinary people by the defaulters; those poor people were promised to be paid a small percentage of the amount transferred in lieu of their accounts being used by the thugs. Now the government has clarified that no withdrawals from such accounts shall be allowed till the Income Tax department scrutinizes such accounts. All such accounts have been sealed at Rupees 50,000 cash deposits only. That again has helped to lessen the people's woes.

"Similarly, huge amounts were being deposited by politicians and others in the bank account of farmers on the pretext that they won't be taxed. But the government, after knowing these facts, has now stopped withdrawals from such accounts where large amounts of money have suddenly been deposited."

Bill: "That is fine; keep that happening. Although my dad did not complain at all, he had to stand in the J&K bank ATM queue today for more than an hour. The machine then malfunctioned just when he reached there. It took the bank another 40 minutes to get it fixed.

The government personnel must put cotton buds in their ears and not be distracted by the negativity coming from the Opposition. All positive energy must be focused on meeting the needs of the common man on the street."

Subash: "The problem with the ATM is the when it works continuously for say an hour...it stops withdrawals, as the machine gets heated up. It then needs a cooling period before it starts again.

The PM is monitoring the events all the time and holding daily meetings with the Finance Ministry, RBI and all concerned. These meetings are targeted to ensure that more and more comfort and convenience is brought forward for the people."

Bill: "This is a master stroke by the government."

Subash: "The next step is more forceful which, however, will involve only the high and mighty...*benami* transaction ban and reviewing of *benami* transactions till date. *Hawala* traders are under the lens and NGOs are allowed no transactions at the present."

Bill: "No backward step now. The government must go for the jugular vein of the corruption, once and for all."

Subash: "Just now watched a TV report from Chandigarh... people say it is business as usual in the SBI bank branches and ATMs as well. They said they could exchange currency, withdraw currency and deposit cash within 5 to 10 minutes. The situation is improving day by day.

The government has allowed Class C&D employees of the Central Govt withdrawal of Rupees 10,000 per month as advance salary, with immediate effect. The government is doing everything possible to make people more and more comfortable.

The black money hoarders are out there to create problems... hiring people to exchange and deposit money...but the government is hell bent to beat their intent."

Bill: "Just go for the jugular of all corruption. It is now or never!"

Subash: "As per the government estimates, more than 80% of the currency printed was in Rupee 500 and 1000 notes. So, the percentage of Rupee 100 currency notes must have been less than 10%. When there is so much demand of the currency, how can one expect Rupee 100 currency notes to be available in plenty. Once the new 500 notes are readily available in the banks...the situation will automatically ease out. It is not an easy job to print, circulate and distribute new currency notes in such a huge country of more than 1.32 billion. The earlier decision to demonetise and now its implementation could not have even been thought by any other leader. Our PM is a risk taker and continues moving ahead the best way he can."

Bill: "Such bold initiatives succeed only if a majority of the population understands the objectives and stands behind you. Thankfully, India's hard working middle class, which comprises more than 50% of the total population, has shown sanity and supported it. The lower 25% of the population struggles to make ends meet. I believe it is the upper 10 to 15% people who are feeling the pinch of this master stroke and crying foul.

The PM made many promises to the people at the time of his election. People then gave him the mandate. His is now obligated to deliver what he had promised. People rule—that is the essence of democracy.

3.2.3.9 Cricket

This chat took place somewhere around 18 November 2016, when Australia was playing against South Africa at home in Australia and India was playing England at home in India.

Bill: "Our cricket team is in crisis."

Subash: "Not at all....it is 208 for 2...for India."

Bill: "I am talking about the Aussies. Remember that I have permanent Aussie stripes over my Indian blues. We are two tests down and that too playing at home—unprecedented. About the Indian team, yes, I am waiting for Pujara and Kohli to score their tons."

Subash: "Australia are playing against SA, I think. *Humara dil toh hai Hindustani...so humko Hindustan hi har jagah dikhta hai,* (I am an Indian and I see India everywhere). It is a game and may the better team win...be it from any country. Let the game win."

Bill: "No, it is cricket. I have never played cricket for a draw or to lose. No statesmanship in cricket; go for the kill. Cricket is modern day's war. I am a soldier; I play to only win. I am not that benevolent. Australia have just lost two tests in a row at home, which is not acceptable. Many heads will roll now, perhaps have already started rolling. To be the best, one must perform and be accountable."

Subash: "Yes, of course, and every team must be thinking on these lines. But irrespective of the situations, we need to back and support our teams. It is unusual for Aussies and they always take remedial actions faster than others."

Bill: "Yes, our team always comes first. Players should always be on their toes and never take their place in the team for granted."

Subash: "But still, the quality and performance of players lets the teams down at times."

Bill: "There is a lot of noise here about our cricket. For some very strange reasons, the team has underperformed. Half the team will be new for the third test. At least five players may be grounded, some players for ever. We have a huge pool of talent. It is just matter of putting together a winning team. Traditionally, Aussies win through the team effort, and not due to one or two master players. The team must gel together fast and start delivering."

Subash: "This happens to every team at one point or the other but Australia is not used to suffering consecutive defeats. Cricket Australia is a very decisive body. That is what it is all about. Gelling of the team together ensures better results."

3.3 AN AUSTRALIAN EXAMPLE OF NATIONALISM

The other day, at about 5.15 am, we saw two fellow morning walkers, both in their early seventies, with their pets waiting nearby, trying to disentangle and remove mistletoes from the branches of a seemingly dying papyrus tree on the river side. It seemed they had also brought with them two long sticks, with forks, to do the job. But they were struggling to reach the higher branches of the tree. It was an awesome show. No one had told them to do so. We asked them why they were doing it themselves when they could contact the local council. They said it was their responsibility too to look after the environment. That is called taking the ownership of your country.

This is not the first time that we have witnessed such an act of active citizenship. It is a common sight to find morning walkers, joggers and runners stopping and picking up rubbish in the parks and footpaths (such as plastic bags, cans and plastic bottles left carelessly by some picnic goers over the weekend) and dispose it of in a designated rubbish bin. This sense of active citizenship and ownership of the country is inborn in most Australians; no wonder Australia has been one of the most liveable countries in the world. This is how many people in Australia look after the local flora and fauna.

Could I imagine such a scene and such selfless sense of public ownership anywhere in India? Perhaps yes, some people in India may be doing exactly what these two ladies did but, unfortunately, not many people would do.

In India, everything must be done by the government. The majority of people in India seem to lack a basic sense of ownership of their country, their city, or their street—be it in terms of paying their income tax or in terms of stark indifference shown by them towards the upkeep of their street or the city, or saving the environment or just solving burning social issues.

The readers should note that only about 40% of Australians work and all of them pay income tax and submit their annual tax returns. That is how the country meets the needs and the social security expenses of the remaining 60% of population. An average middle class worker pays up to about 40% of income in terms of Income Tax, GST and annual Council and Water fees.

Chapter 4
Winter of 2016 – Demonetisation

4.0 TRUE NATIONALISM

6th December 2016, 6.00 am.

International Terminal (T3), IGIA, Delhi.

I was relieved that my Singapore Airlines flight landed on time, at 5.25 am, in relatively friendlier weather conditions. A couple of days earlier, many flights from Delhi airport had reportedly either been cancelled or diverted to other airports due to dense morning fog in the Delhi airport area.

As usual, I needed to convert my Australian currency into Indian currency for meeting my daily expenses during my 10 day stay in India. A very long queue at the Punjab National Bank booth inside the terminal building made me quite anxious and a little nervous. It would have taken me at least two hours to reach the window and potentially at that time be advised that the booth had run out of cash. Two Thomas Cook booths were already out of cash. So, I decided to leave the terminal building and take a shuttle bus to Terminal 1D, as my Jammu flight was scheduled at 8.50 am. Outside the building, another Thomas Cook booth had a long queue of new arrivals crawling towards its window. So, without any Indian rupees in my pocket, I decided to take a shuttle bus to domestic terminal 1D.

The shuttle bus, scheduled to leave at 6.15 am, was delayed. I became a little nervous and restless. I asked a waiting fellow passenger, in his early 30s, standing at Bay no 10, if he was also heading to Terminal 1D. Seeing his inability to communicate in English, I translated my question into Hindi.

He replied, "Sir, I am going to Varanasi. I have just arrived from Kuwait. By the way, where are you going? If you feel so anxious, why don't you take a taxi to Terminal 1D?"

I said, "I am going to Jammu. I can't taxi a taxi because I don't have even a single Indian rupee. Didn't you see such a long queue waiting outside the PNB booth inside the terminal?"

To my pleasant surprise, he said, "Sir, I can give you some cash. Please take a taxi."

I said, "Thank you, but it won't be required if the shuttle bus arrives soon. However, if it is delayed, I may request you to give me some taxi money. In that case, we can travel together to Terminal 1D."

He said, "Sir, that is fine. But you can still keep some Indian currency as you may need it till you reach home. I have no problem in giving it to you."

I said, "I am meeting my wife at Terminal 1D; she is also travelling to Jammu with me. She may have some Indian currency with her."I continued, "You are a very kind person, you don't even know me and you are offering me money."

He said, "Sir, I come from a poor family. I am not a graduate but I like to help others. In Kuwait, I normally help many people from India, Pakistan, Bangladesh and other countries who need any help."

"That makes you a very rich person. You have a big and rich heart. Many people have lots of wealth but may not be as rich as you are. By the way, I didn't even ask your name," I asked with curiosity.

"Sir, my name is Atiq Ahmad. I come from a village in Azamgarh, near Varanasi. My parents are dead. I was married a year ago. My wife is waiting for me at home," he replied excitedly in pure Hindi. "I bake naan bread in various restaurants in Kuwait," he continued. Thereupon, I also introduced myself—my family, my Kashmiri origins and the present country of my residence etc. I also informed him that I had authored two books, both of which were in the process of being published, and that I was in the process of writing my third book. I promised him that I would mention his kind gesture in one book. He was impressed and noted the name of my books in his diary and promised to read them when published.

After a few minutes, I saw a shuttle bus coming towards our bus terminal. I had just a hand bag and a laptop bag to carry, so I offered Atiq my help with loading of one of his two large, new, polyethylene wrapped, red suitcases onto the shuttle bus, which he accepted reluctantly. The 20-minute journey to the domestic airport seemingly finished in a jiffy as we continued our chat in the bus. Upon reaching Terminal 1D, I also offloaded one of his two suitcases and he sounded so grateful. Finally, after exchanging a warm hug, we went our separate ways. He was a good man by every measure.

After my initial security check, no sooner had I joined the queue in front of the checking counters of Go Airlines, that I noticed my wife, Rekha, walking towards me. She had a deep blue mark right under her left eye, which she tried to cover with makeup. Reportedly, she had suffered a nasty fall at an NCERT building where she had made a business presentation a few days ago.

After our security check, we settled for breakfast at one of the open cafes in the departure lounge, which appeared to be quite impressive, with a large number of shops and eating places.

The food was delicious, and thankfully did not pose any health threats. The rates were international.

Our boarding took place right on time, as Go Air, as well as other leading airlines in India, are known for their punctuality. However, with its air-conditioner blowing cold air at full throttle, the plane did not take off at the scheduled time. The captain made an announcement on the PA system that the take-off was delayed by up to 20 minutes as a VIP was flying out of Delhi, possibly to attend the funeral of the Tamil Nadu Chief Minister, Jayalalithaa, who had just passed on.

About 20 minutes after the scheduled time, the plane finally took off. It was a smooth 70 minute flight to Jammu. Courtesy our travel agent at Jammu, we were served with a complimentary breakfast (vegetarian sandwiches and pomegranate juice) aboard the plane.

After a smooth landing at the Jammu airport, which is manned by Indian Air force, we were received by my dad. On my request, before reaching home, we first rushed to the Hari Market branch of State Bank of India (SBI) for buying some Indian currency. We found the bank staff very courteous and helpful.

4.1 SHALLOW SOCIAL RELATIONS

I visited our relatives to meet my father-in-law who had shifted there for a few days. It seemed our visit was not important for the host, as he kept himself visibly busy with his work during our two-hour visit. This is not the first time that my relative showed such a carefree, rather a little discourteous behaviour. In the past couple of years, he may have visited my Jammu home at the most a couple of times during my frequent, but short visits. I recall, exactly a year ago, he did not even honour a couple of lunch invitations at my home, one of these being on my dad's birthday in December 2015. On the contrary, I visited his home at least two to three during each visit to Jammu.

Perhaps due to high frequency of my visits, people don't seem to care if I have to undertake a long journey to reach Jammu and catch-up with them after covering a distance of about 11,000 km, first over the Indian Ocean and then over the Indian landmass, via three flights, with the cumulative flying time in the air of about 12 hours; not to speak of a significant cost of flights—in terms of dollars, precious time and immense physical discomfort.

With each visit, my feeling has become stronger that my acquaintances and relatives don't really care whether they meet me or not. Whether I have been in Jammu all the time since they saw me last or if I have been overseas between the meetings. Such a feeling can be extrapolated to a stark realisation—people don't care if I am living or if am dead.

People's behaviour at Jammu was not always like this. During my initial return visits to Jammu in the late 1990s, after my emigration in early 1995, many people would keenly visit us after knowing that we had just arrived. We would also visit many relatives, friends and acquaintances to catch up. There used to be many lunches and dinners on both sides, lots of interaction and catching up, and exchange of stories from either side. But all that has disappeared over the years. I can attribute people's attitude and behaviour to some very obvious factors:

- We have lost the novelty and surprise element. During the past couple of decades, I have not grown a tail at my back or horns on my head; I still look more or less the same and wear the same wrist watch (Seiko 5 Automatic), which my father gave me when I was 15.
- We have been very frugal in carrying gifts for people from overseas. The reasons are that many recipients in the past either did not show any excitement on receiving them or downgraded them saying India had better things to offer.
- In practical terms, we have lost much of our utility for the local residents of Jammu. We don't have important contacts or local authority which they could exploit for their benefit. Simply, we have no use for them, as we have nothing much to offer; so why waste time on us?
- We live a relatively much simpler lifestyle and carry simpler thoughts, as a result of living overseas for the past two decades or so. Simplicity seems to be out of fashion in India. Many Indians are very fashion conscious and tech savvy. Therefore, many people possibly perceive us as old fashioned.

4.2 MY WILL

In the light of perceived complications about funerals and how bothersome and expensive one's death has become over time for one's family members, in terms of money, logistics and time, I had a discussion with my family at home one day at breakfast, when I announced my will as follows.

- When I die, my body should be cremated at the place where my body is found on the planet and then my ashes be brought to Kashmir and scattered (not buried) on the grassed high slopes of Pahalgam, in the company of devdar trees (conifers), at the feet of Amaranth.

- No mourning should be observed on any day after my death. No traditional Kashmiri Pandit last rites, such as the 10th, 11th or 12th days to be performed by any priest.

For environmental reasons, I don't want any river or a water body in India, or anywhere else in the world, to be polluted with my ashes or with anything that results from my funeral.

4.3 BRAVE & GUTSY ENGINEERS

During my visit, I visited my friend, Vijay Raina[46], at his office at Gandhi Nagar. He was my classmate in our Bachelor's degree course in Civil Engineering at REC Srinagar. Surprisingly, his Chief Engineer, Mr Rasheed[47], two levels above Vijay, was also our classmate. I wondered how the system allowed two engineers from the same batch, and the same university, to be in that hierarchal situation. It must be extremely frustrating, discouraging and disconcerting for Vijay to find himself two levels below his classmate. The irony does not end there; a couple of our juniors at the college, whom I also met at the office, were one level above Vijay. It is not very hard to imagine how disheartening it must have been for Vijay to see himself stuck in his position with others surpassing him. Vijay would be retiring in just another five to six years from the government service!

In my honest opinion, with my life in an anti-discriminatory country like Australia, this situation is extremely annoying, thanks to India's system of reservations, which allows a part of her society to enjoy a disproportionately high level of privileges. I patted myself on my back for having left this country and such a discriminatory system.

Marginalisation and discrimination based on one's background is akin to a severe curse, whether it is marginalisation of the people belonging to so-called backward and underprivileged communities or marginalisation of the people belonging to the remaining communities. In this instance, this is a clear case of state-supported marginalisation

---

46 Name changed for confidentiality purposes.

47 Name changed for confidentiality purposes.

and discrimination against the people belonging to the mainstream (accrual to a reverse discrimination).

For the upliftment of a society as a whole, to a reasonable extent, I do support conditional reservation of the existing quota system for admissions to tertiary education institutions and employment in government departments for the people belonging to the backward and underprivileged communities but only for one generation of any family. In no case, do I support any unconditional continuation of enjoyment of such privileges (reserved quota) by any subsequent generations. It is not fair for the people belonging to the mainstream. If one generation of a family does well, thanks to the reservations in quotas in admission, or jump-starting a government job or fast-tracking promotions at work, all privileges under that category must cease for all future generations of that family; they should then be considered in the mainstream. If all future generations of that family continue enjoying such state-supported privileges, that will be tantamount to continuation of clear discrimination against the people of the mainstream.

During my two hour stay at Vijay's office, the so-called technical group was busy discussing a solution to address malfunctioning of a sluice gate in a hydroelectric project dam. Instead of discussing possible technical solutions, they seemed to discuss the blame game and how to get around the problem with least damage to any one of them. The way these people work in the country is against common sense and contradicts good engineering practices that are followed in Australia and other developed countries.

On probing, Vijay said that a particular bureaucrat and a connected politician had decided not to promote a certain group of people, including him, as long as they did not pay like others did. Somehow, this group of engineers had decided to forego their promotions but not to pay a cent. Brave engineers indeed!

In that system, it needs guts to stand up to corrupt officials and politicians. If only every engineer was like them, one would see better infrastructure development in terms of the overall quality of the construction, speed of the construction and the maintenance works.

4.4 MINDLESS WEDDINGS

A friend, Dr Sunil Bhat, asked me if I was a social scientist, or a leader, or an authority to call for an urgent reform in the Indian wedding ceremonies.

I said I was none of these but, as a responsible member of the Kashmiri Indian community, albeit living overseas, I saw it as my responsibility that I should try to educate people from my community in India and urge them to undertake necessary reforms for their own good.

He further asked, "You are a normal person, how come you think like this? Is there any such precedence set by any social leader? If people are happy doing what they do, what is the problem with you? Let them do what they feel like."

This kind of challenge was not unexpected. I had met many other educated and responsible people from India who had challenged my concern in a more or less similar manner.

I replied, "Sunil, you really want to know what my problem is if people want to spend money on their lavish weddings; after all it is their money. It is madness, in my honest opinion."

And this is how I explained:

The traditions

In India, people blame their traditions and culture for organising the wedding ceremonies of their children and close family members. Little do they know that their culture has never stopped changing and evolving! If they do a little homework, look at the family albums, or listen to the older members of their community or their grandparents (or great grandparents, if are they fortunate enough to have them around), it won't take them much time to learn that the culture of their ancestors differed significantly from the present culture that they are talking about.

Growing up in Kashmir, I did not see much change in the style and the size of the wedding ceremonies till I left Kashmir in Dec 1989, except that some families had started introducing buffet style wedding reception lunches from about the mid-eighties. Perhaps that was out of compulsion due to lack of space or not many younger people being available to serve the traditional sit down dinner or lunch. After their migration from Kashmir, the Pandits had to rely on commercial wedding resorts and marriage halls. So, that marked the introduction of a new hybrid culture.

Menu

The menu has also expanded phenomenally. Instead of sticking to a typical pre-migration era menu, they have added many courses in the last quarter of a century, which were previously alien to them, such as from Punjab, Gujarat, South India, South-East Asia and Europe.

Serving alcohol, although clandestinely in most cases, has become a common norm now due to the expectations of the relatives and friends. No one is actually thinking—why should the host serve free alcohol?

Rituals

Even the rituals have not been spared. The traditional *pooja* seems to be highly compromised. Not many people pay attention to the Vedic Mantras that are supposed to be recited during a Hindu wedding.

The priest is bribed to shorten the duration of the Vedic rituals, from traditional seven to eight hours to less than three hours, with the remaining time being spent on the photo sessions. The professional photographer rules the roost. We have been witness to a wedding ceremony where the priest and the photographer nearly exchanged blows. The photographer started giving instructions to the priest how a particular ritual should be performed and the latter retorted and asked him to shut up and mind his own business.

In the *jaimala*[48] ceremony, which marks a post 1990-migration addition for the Kashmiri Pandit wedding ceremonies, the bride

---

48 *Jaimala*' means 'victory garland'. The word '*jai*' means victory and the word '*mala*' means a garland. The term '*varmala*' is also used interchangeably with the term '*jaimala*'; the word 'var' means the groom.

In the Hindu epic Ramayana, Sita garlanded Rama after he strung Shiva's bow at her *swayamvara*. Since then, the practice has continued in many Indian cultures in the form of *jaimala* ritual, wherein the bride places a flower garland over her intended groom and the groom reciprocates.

and the groom are supposed to place garlands around each other's neck, gently and with dignity, to mark each other's acceptance. This new ceremony was originally alien to Kashmiris. The latest fashion is to make the yet-to-be-wedded couple climb flimsy ladders to reach a high level revolving platform, about 3 to 5 m above the ground, where they are handed the garlands for performing the *jaimala* ceremony, by a drone which circles above their head. In one such case, the platform collapsed and, unfortunately, killed the bride-to-be.

The bride and the groom are raised high by their friends and relatives during the exchange of garlands, to make it difficult for them to put the garland around each other's neck. This new ritual provides a thrill and show for all present around the couple, albeit on a vulgar side. Some people abhor seeing it but keep quiet for being ridiculed by the host.

I am not overly concerned about the decency associated with raising a groom by supporting his hips and buttocks; I feel utterly disappointed, rather ashamed, to see a bride being raised by her young friends and relatives, especially when she is wearing a flimsy wedding dress. Where is the decency left? Does this act not outrage the modesty of a woman? Where has the bride's modesty gone? To my shock, I see every one present around laughing and smiling while this 'vulgar' act is being enacted. I am sure you will agree with me that this is not Kashmiri Indian culture. Is anyone thinking?

Imagine the scene from the eyes of an Indian Kashmiri who lives overseas. Here in Australia, the wedding ceremonies are so well organised, without any fuss or noise. How dignified the wedding couple look! In particular, the bride looks like a fairy, walking down

---

Traditionally in India, the victorious Indian kings and princes, returning home alive from the battlefield, would be greeted with a *jaimala*. In the North Indian weddings, the wedding procession (*baraat*) that accompanies the groom is seen as the war procession. In Kashmir, the groom is called *maharaaza* (means 'maharaja'–an emperor). As soon as he disembarks from his specially decorated car or, in many cases, these days dismounts from his horse, he is instantly garlanded by the bride's family.

the aisle with her father, with bridesmaids behind her. There are speeches by the family members and friends; and people attending the ceremony know exactly what is happening. Everyone attending the wedding feels honoured to have made it to the list of the selected bunch of attendees. The sacred marriage vows are taken in the presence of all important relatives and friends, unlike in India, where not many people pay attention to the actual wedding ceremonies; it has now become mainly a photographic session.

Noise

Not to speak of the noise in the Indian weddings! It is really deafening and irritating if one is eating food. This is the product of a new cultural evolution, without much thought, of course. The wedding organisers play the latest Bollywood and folk music at a deafening volume level on those big speakers. During one such reception, in November 2015, at Jammu, I remember requesting the hostess at least four times to ask the musicians to lower the volume of the music (rather noise). Each time, the hostess nodded her head, somewhat puzzled, and walked to the DJ (disk jockey). For a couple of minutes the volume sounded a shade lower only to become louder than ever again. Perhaps, I was the only gutsy person in that gathering of about 300 people who dared to do so, maybe based on my Australian enculturation and forthrightness. So many people, especially the elderly ones, looked visibly irritated, but no one dared to complain, obviously for political correctness.

Chaos

In Indian weddings, many guests don't even know their host who is paying for their food. If one is not formally introduced to the host or the hostess, generally one wouldn't even be able to identify them in that loud and relatively overcrowded atmosphere. In many cases, I happened to attend a wedding because my father was invited (with family) and I happened to be visiting him at that point of time. I didn't know anyone at the wedding party. On many such occasions, I have felt very guilty devouring the free food. I also figured that I had no reason to be there except that I accompanied my father who felt obligated to be there. My dad always introduces me to the host. On learning that I am visiting from overseas, the host invariably gives me a little more special treatment by ordering the waiters to fill my plate, and even introduces me to the newlyweds, where a professional photographer is usually ready to instruct me to pose for a picture with them. Everything happens in a mechanistic sequence. After a couple of hours I leave with my dad, wondering why I have been there at all.

Food

Let us again talk about food. Due to fast growing affluence in the last few decades, coupled with low physical activities and abundance of television channels, many people have put on weight beyond their healthy weight range and a considerable number of people are on regular medication after they develop Type 2 diabetes, hypertension and other associated physical ailments. Nearly half the affluent population appears to be overweight and many people are obese. So, when such people partake of the rich food that is commercially cooked and served in the wedding ceremonies, one cannot help but wonder at their careless attitude. It seems these obese people don't care about their health or probably believe their medication will fix everything. On many occasions, I have wondered about the purpose of serving unhealthy food to a considerable percentage of people who are already on medication and, therefore, must not consume that kind of food. At times, I have been shocked to see some known diabetics serving themselves two to three scoops of ice-cream.

In addition, a lot of wastage of food takes place. Many people greedily serve themselves much more food that they can possibly consume, which results in considerable food wastage. Interestingly, it is not unusual to see people thronging in close proximity to the food stalls while standing and eating. I have never been able to understand such behaviour. Perhaps they fear the stalls may suddenly close down or disappear, or perhaps the food might be finished by other guests. Such is the competition in eating the free party food! Many people appear to eat out of greed, perhaps with some subconscious sense of insecurity and past poverty.

One day, in Feb 2017, I called my dad to enquire how he was doing after attending a wedding reception the night before at Hotel Hari Palace, which is one of my favourite places in Jammu. The hotel complex is located atop a hill on the bank of River Tawi. It has a large and beautiful, green turfed, outdoor sitting area where I like to relax for a couple of hours during my visit to Jammu and unwind away from the city din. Although my personal food consumption remains very limited outside home in India, being a vegan vegetarian, I like the setting and the service with a smile, offered by this place. Apparently, that night my dad had enjoyed himself at the reception party. Before I could ask him anything, he kept going, "I did not eat the main meal. I ate a variety of snacks, which filled me up." Then, he updated me with a long list of snacks that were served at the party, as well as the main dinner menu. He boasted that he was feeling very well despite eating at the party. Being health conscious, he had been very careful in his selection, as well as the quantity that he had eaten. And I did believe him; he is never greedy with food. I asked him if other guests and his relatives had also limited their food intake to snacks only. He laughed and said, "No, they all ate the full meal even after eating the full range of snacks." This did not surprise me, as I could imagine and clearly see the picture, from my earlier memories, about how some of my relatives would have enjoyed themselves at the party.

If we count in terms of calories, an average person consumes at least 3,000 to 5,000 kCal during each lunch or dinner party.

From the health point of view, a sedentary person (note that most people in India have a sedentary lifestyle, especially the women) should limit the daily intake of calories to 1,500 per day, whereas a moderate worker can consume up to around 2,000 kCal a day. Therefore, it is hard to estimate that on a party day, an average person consumes up to three times the suggested daily intake of calories, which means an extra 3,500 kCal, which equates to about 300 gm of fat. In a typical wedding season, an average person attends at least five to ten such wedding parties, which results in an extra weight gain of 1.5 to 3.0 kg. In ten years, this weight gain equates to15 to 30 kg, i.e. a person become first overweight and then obese. What does it mean?

It means development of Type 2 diabetes, hypertension, bone, spine and muscle issues and numerous other permanent ailments. So, is it worth it? Affluence and intake of rich food equate with disease and a shortened life!

Wedding Cost

How much should a wedding cost? Well, in the simplest forms, a legal wedding should not cost more than a few hundred rupees, which may include the following costs:

- registration fee at a marriage registrar's office or a court;
- a couple of hundred rupees to a priest, as *dakshana,* to perform a simple Vedic ceremony at a local temple;
- cost of two fresh flower garlands; and
- cost of a simple cup of tea, with samosa and a laddu, each for the newlyweds and their closest friends and family members.

If pride and showing-off in the garb of social obligations, customs and traditions, would not be in the equation, an average wedding should cost less than a thousand rupees. This would ensure that millions of parents did not have to lose their sleep, and their integrity while accepting and giving bribes, in accumulating the kind of wealth they need to fund the wedding ceremonies of their children.

Let us see how much do the wedding ceremonies typically cost the middle class Indians. Based on my general observations at Jammu, a typical Kashmiri Pandit wedding comprises two to three main functions. In each of those functions, food is catered for between 200 to 400 people. So, assuming food is to be provided for 600 people on average, with each plate costing around Rupees 1,000 on the average, the cost of the food alone would be around Rupees 600,000. To this, one must add Rupees 200,000 to 400,000 as the cost of renting the marriage home and decorations for a few days. If we include the costs of the gifts, jewellery, expensive clothing, videography/ photography, DJ etc. (say Rupees 800,000), the average cost of an average Indian wedding would, therefore, be around Rupees 1,600,000 to 1,800,000. However, I have heard many people saying that a wedding costs Rupees 2,000,000 to 2,500,000 on average, but that could be an inflated figure[49].So, a person having two children to marry off will have to look at wedding expenses of around Rupees 4,000,000.

In the current scenario, if the average monthly salary of a person is Rupees 50,000, it will take him at least 80 months (i.e. around 6.6 years) to save that kind of money, assuming his partner is able to meet all other running expenses related to the home, allowing Rupees 35,000 with strict controls on the expenses and without any holidays. Now, suppose it is a single income family, it will take them around 265 months (about 22 years) to save that kind of money, barring inflation.

Does it make sense to blitz one's hard earned savings in the passage of one week? And to whose benefit? The newlyweds don't benefit, neither do the guests. In fact, the greedy guests are disadvantaged—they become unhealthier and need extra medication to pay for their eating sins and their greed in partaking of unhealthy food. The only people who benefit are the service providers. Most of the gold jewellery and expensive clothing generally remains unused a few months after the wedding.

Has it become the mission of one's life to save every rupee that one can, only to burn it quickly, mindlessly, after a few years? People don't go for holidays; they try to save every penny that they can for meeting such wedding expenses. They bargain with the vendor every time they buy fruit and vegetables; some even walk a kilometre or more to save five rupees. There are many people who spend that kind of money but don't even own a decent set of cutlery at their home. A few years ago, it took my host nearly five minutes to find me a decent fork and a spoon to eat my dinner at their home. Eventually, I had to eat my lunch with an old dented aluminium tea spoon. The family boasted of numerous electronic gadgets and facilities, which

---

49 A close friend recently told me that he had spent about Rupees 3,000,000 on the wedding of his daughter and swore me to confidentiality. However, based on the total number of guests that had attended the wedding over that week and the cost of each food plate (which he himself shared with me), I worked out that he had inflated the figure by about two times. He would not have spent more than Rupees 800,000 on the food and arrangements and say another Rupees 700,000 on jewellery etc., the total cost of the wedding would have been under Rupees 1,500,000.

included a video camera, which the gentleman would show-off at all social events (weddings), wearing designer clothes.

Upon hearing my long explanation, Sunil still did not feel convinced. He asked gently, "But, if people are happy spending that kind of money, what is your problem? They can afford to do so because they have enough."

I replied, "You are talking about a decent middle class family. The middle class has a wide range of income, although people socialise together. The families which form the bulk of middle class sit within the 'lower end to middle' of the middle class range. Just because they socialise with people belonging to the upper range, they attract unnecessary social pressure upon themselves because their next of kin or a close relative can afford a relatively lavish wedding or any other social function. We belong to a community which believes in showing-off to prove we are no less than other people. I remember my grandfather saying that his first cousin, who was not very well-off, would smear some turmeric around his lips to show that he had had a hearty meal. I remember many people would wear freshly washed and ironed collars, not shirts, during the winter months in Kashmir, as it was easier to wash and iron a collar instead of a proper short.

People would also reverse the collar of their old worn out shirts at their tailor's shop after one side of the collar would be frayed. People would stitch holes in their socks to keep using them.

Most households try to save every penny that they possibly can, with an aim to meet the heavy expenses related to the education of their children, including private tuitions and capitation fee at private colleges or universities; sickness and disease; construction of their new house or repairs; modification to their existing homes; and the weddings of their children. Of these, apart from the construction of a new house, the wedding expenses form the largest household expenditure. But this expenditure is unique in the sense that it cannot be termed as any investment whatsoever, whereas the other named expenditures are necessary for the well-being of the family members, their health, education and professional career and, therefore, can be termed as investments, with tangible returns on the investments. However, in the case of a wedding, other than the purchase of gold ornaments, most of the expenses can reasonably be deemed to be non-essential. It looks as if the hosts have been working all their lives and saving money for the owner of the marriage home or resort.

In essence, in practical terms, the host appears to serve relatively rich and unhealthy food to guests, a considerable number of whom are on the diabetic and hypertension medication. It is not unusual that the guests who have devoured the food leave the party criticising the arrangement or the quality of the food itself, or whine about the poor service or lack of personalised attention from the host/hostess. Also the failure rate of marriages has recently risen at an alarming rate so there is no guarantee that a marriage being performed will actually survive the test of time due to individual ego clashes, personal independence, unreasonable burden of expectations from one or both sides, extramarital relationships etc. On average, two to three marriages fail within about two years after the wedding. So, who other than the owners of marriage halls or resorts or hotels benefit from such weddings?

So, does it really make any sense in this day and age that the present day literate and educated middle class people in India burn their earnings of decades in a matter of few days, and to what purpose? What do they really achieve, other than a tick in a box, in the social context, that they have also performed the wedding in accordance with the fashion of the day?

It is heard that most Indian families live for the day of the wedding of their children, as if it is the ultimate goal of their lives.

Humans are known to be social animals. It won't be wrong, however, to say that humans are also herd animals. Their herd mentality is very apparent in India, in particular with regard to the performance of the weddings. The herd mentality does not allow many people to think independently. Everyone seems to follow someone, who could be a friend or a close relative, while also competing with that person without questioning themselves why they really do what they are doing? A blind race, it seems! People have a sickening tendency to show-off (in the guise of '*shauk*') to their own best friends and close relatives, on whom they rely emotionally, that they are no less than anyone and can afford to perform the wedding of their child in a 'grand' manner, which will be 'remembered' by all for everyone times to come. There is always going to be another grander function by someone else. The race never ends. With each wedding, there is something new to show-off, be it in terms of food items, or decoration, or the venue itself. Unfortunately, many people, with lesser resources, become victims of this mindless show-off race driven by the people of higher socio-economic groups.

Little do people realise that human memory is very short. People come, eat and go. In an Indian wedding season, people go from one wedding party to another in a matter of a few hours. All they look for is a good time. How many people really care how much money you actually spent or how grand your wedding was? After their belly is full, it is time for coffee, followed by a *pan* or a *supari* and then they leave the party, with a satisfied smile on their face, leaving the poor host counting the bills. Within a few hours only, a wedding party is practically forgotten by most guests. It is only the host or hostess who are left to rue their thoughtless and stupid spending and that too for seemingly a thankless task. Their frustration increases significantly when they realise that they are now left with a thinner financial cushion for their own old age, to meet the associated everyday living needs, sickness, disease etc. To add salt to their wounds, in many cases, their own children practically wash their hands off from any responsibility towards them. So, it becomes a case of loss-loss, i.e. losing at both ends—losing savings on one end (which can be prevented) and losing their children with time (which is inevitable in many cases).

It is evident that many people are not even aware that weddings can be performed in a much simpler, yet dignified fashion, and at a cost which could be a fraction of the costs they incur at the present.

In the process, they could also be absolutely free to reclaim their lives and enjoy the journey by way of frequent holidays and lesser compromises on their spending on numerous activities that can potentially enhance the quality of their lives.

I recently attended a wedding in Perth between a young cardiologist of Indian origin and his Australian girlfriend. The wedding ceremony was a much simpler affair than typical Indian weddings. All expenses of the wedding, followed by a decent wedding reception, were borne by the groom. What a forward looking and progressive young man. It is not surprising that the groom's father is a decorated Indian Air force officer, recipient of Mahavir Chakra in 1971 Indo-Pak war. He beamed with joy and looked so proud of his illustrious son. Can others follow in this young man's footsteps?

4.5 AN ALTERNATIVE MODEL

Without losing sight of the basic objectives of a wedding, and in light of the inherent human search for personal freedom and independence, it would be pragmatic to keep the wedding function as simple as possible, albeit strongly upholding the sanctity of the whole affair.

What is that sanctity?

That sanctity is the mutual trust. It is founded on mutual respect between the two people, which then translates formally into an expressed commitment from both to live together and support each other, through thick and thin, in presence of their immediate family members and their closest friends and relatives. Once the two people take a public vow to dedicate themselves to each other, whilst maintaining their respective dignity and, most importantly, freedom of thought and action, a marriage is complete.

Such a marriage must not cost anything. But, we have complicated the matter over the past few decades, as a result of growing prosperity in the country and the inherent tendency of the Indian people to show off. People have, unfortunately, been resorting to the theory of 'beg, borrow or steal' in order to be able to host lavish weddings. There seems be a rat race; to what, only God knows? Who suffers in the process? The country suffers, through corruption; as also the poorer sections of the society, who have to keep up with the upper strata.

Why can't we have a wedding ceremony which is funded equally by both parties and organised at a shared common venue, which is equally accessible to both parties with relative ease and without any undue disadvantage to any one of the two.

The wedding function could comprise a two-pronged programme:

- The basic wedding ritual performed at a place of worship or at home or a public venue, attended by the closest 15 to 20 people from either family, in an environment characterised by peace and quiet, with full respect for the traditions and complete focus on the ritual itself, without any undue distraction from the cameramen.

- A common reception lunch or dinner for at the most 100 people from each side, hosted jointly by the two parties who would also equally share the total cost of the whole wedding.

The above model would serve the following objectives:

- Social equality between the two families would be displayed by bringing them on parity with each other. No party would feel less than the other; both would effectively host each other.
- Gender bias would be effectively addressed and eliminated, once and for all, once more and more people adopt this model. The bride and the bride's family would be able to stand tall and walk shoulder to shoulder with the groom and his family.
- It would be like a marriage of the two families and not only the two individuals. Once that happens, the larger family would provide a solid united support to the two people, emotionally, physically and financially, which is very important in this day and age when a significant number of newly married couples divorce each other after a short period of time.
- It will also bond the two families effectively for ever, as neither would feel any kind of pressure to keep serving the other. Happiness and fulfilment will prevail.
- The newly married couple and their immediate families would benefit. A significant amount of money could be saved by both families, which could then be used by them for meeting a number of more essential expenditures.
- The nation would benefit. As the total cost of a wedding would be significantly low, it could then be easily manageable with normal savings from a regular salary. Accordingly, a forced corruption practice, which is currently rampant across the nation to acquire the kind of money that is needed for lavish weddings, would effectively be stopped.
- Happiness levels would rise across the nation. The kind of mental stress that people carry lifelong worrying about their child's wedding, especially the costs of the wedding

ceremony, dowry and gifts etc., silently impacts the health of many parents. They age much faster and die earlier than their counterparts in Europe and other western countries.

- The current shameful and heartbreaking female foeticide practice in the country, especially in the northern states of India, would stop.

Only once all this happens, the people will deserve to shout *Jai Mata Di* at the top of their voices. Otherwise, this is only a hollow slogan and does not mean anything.

CHAPTER 5
Spring 2017 – An Unusual Dream Sequence

5.0 WELCOME TO DELHI

To mark my first trip of the year, I landed at Delhi towards the end of March 2017. Spring was in air, but a little warmer and seemingly tending towards a hot summer waiting in the wings. I expect at least two more visits to India later this year. My last visit to India, in December 2016, was just a little over four months ago.

India has not looked any different during this trip. As expected, the traffic looks a little heavier than before, obviously because India adds nearly 53,000 vehicles every day to her roads. People look busier as ever and go hurriedly going about their business. Summer seemed to have set in a little earlier than before.

My first day during this trip was very busy and tiring. I felt fatigued and jet lagged after a long travel. Plus, due to the time difference between Perth and Delhi, my eyes started burning by the time dinner was served at my host's home at Delhi, around 9.30 pm local time. My biological clock read the time as12 midnight, in line with the Perth time.

When I hit the bed in my room at the guest house of Engineers Bhawan[50], around midnight local time, I must have quickly dozed off. Next I remember waking up in a dream world. However, at that time, it looked very real. There are times when we can't really differentiate between a dream and the real world. Many dreams appear to be very real; it was one of those. It was also contrastingly different to the world that I had seen earlier in the day.

5.1 A BEAUTIFUL DREAM

I saw myself walking through one of the main streets of Ali Kadal, in downtown Srinagar, Kashmir. The setting was very close to the location of the famous shrine of Resh Peer sahib. In the real world, however, I have not been there in the last 30 years or so. My family ancestral home was located not far from the street where I saw myself walking in my dream. The street looked very neat and the brick walls looked painted with red brick colour. Interestingly, not many people seemed to walk down the street. As in the past, vegetables and fruit vendors and other shops were open on both sides of the street but the number of shoppers and pedestrians looked lesser than I remember from my childhood, perhaps half of that.

I saw bright and young school children, both boys and girls, in their smart school uniforms, walking through the street, with radiant smiles on their faces. They looked curiously towards me.

A child suddenly stopped near a public tap and started drinking water using his right hand as a cup, the same way as I used to drink water from that public tap in my childhood. Those days, tap water used to taste good, cold and refreshing, occasionally chlorinated during the rainy seasons. I don't recall ever falling sick due to the consumption of that water. I remember my parents telling me that the water in our area was sourced from the Sarband, located at Harwan, adjacent to Zabarwan Hills.

On both sides of the street, which looked much wider and cleaner than I had ever seen in my childhood, about 30 years ago, white lines of lime powder were visible, perhaps as a welcome gesture, as is

---

50 The Institution of Engineers (India), Delhi.

customary in Kashmir. Lime powder not only demarcates a boundary, but also helps to get rid of bad odour, and slimy insects and flies, as part of sanitation. An open drain to one side of the street was seen flowing freely and seemed to carry relatively clearer water, with hardly any junk in it; perhaps all the junk had been disposed of separately.

As it happens in a dream, the next moment I saw myself flanked by a number of local, phiran clad people who hugged me, one by one. We all walked towards the old, timber trussed, Ali Kadal Bridge over River Jhelum[51]. I felt I had never left the area; the scene looked as it used to be in the past. Instead of crossing the bridge, we took the cobbled stone steps to the left side of the bridge abutment, to climb downstairs towards the *ghat,* where a happy looking boatman greeted us with a warm smile and helped us to board his waiting boat, which was decorated with garlands of marigold flowers and colourful buntings. I settled on a cushioned white seat on the boat and suddenly realised the water level in the river looked much higher than I had observed during my last trip in July 2016. (These days the river looks significantly silted up, with not much water flowing through it.)The water looked very clean, just like the good old days. Out of curiosity, I dipped my right hand into the water and scooped up some river water in the palm. It was a very refreshing and nostalgic feeling; the water looked very clean and cool, without any floating debris.

As the boatman pushed the boat away from the *ghat*, many other boatpeople (*hanjis*)—children, women and men—standing on the *ghat* started waving. They looked cheerful. Soon, we arrived at a much wider *ghat*, with proper stone cobbled steps, where many people received us.

Going by the events, I felt as if I was some kind of visiting VIP. Soon, I heard myself addressing this gathering of nearly a hundred people in the Kashmiri language. "We will work hard together to make our home beautiful again. We'll restore the dignity and glory of our *MojKashir*[52]. Our land will be the most peaceful place on the

---

51 Known as *Vitasta* in Sanskrit (and Rigveda), or simply *Vyeth* in Kashmiri. The ancient Greeks regarded the river as a god and called it *Hydaspes.* It originates from Verinag Spring in Kashmir. It flows through Srinagar in the Kashmir valley and the Wular Lake before entering Pakistan through a deep narrow gorge at Uri. It has a total length of about 725 kilometres.

52 Kashmiri for 'Mother Kashmir'

earth. We'll all live in harmony and brotherhood, just like we and our ancestors lived in the past. We are all related to one another by blood. We are all one people. We'll fulfil all our dreams together." All the people rallied behind me, "Yes, yes! Inshallah!"

Again, as it often happens in dreams, the next moment I saw myself standing atop a hill overlooking the valley, still accompanied by the same people who had received me earlier. They just followed me. Down below and across, the valley seemed to be covered with a thin layer of white clouds but with many clear patches in between. I saw the top portions of numerous mosques and many temples protruding upwards and shining through the clouds.

Suddenly, the whole place was abuzz with numerous *Aazaan* calls and loud temple bells, as if ringing and singing in a chorus. It all sounded so sweet to my ears. I wept tears of joy, which I could not control. When I turned around, I saw through a hazy gaze that all those *phiran* clad Kashmiris standing with me were happily crying as well. We all shed tears of joy. Many people came close to me and hugged me tightly. Some kissed me on my head, some on my forehead and some on my cheek. Many people patted me on my back. And with that I suddenly woke up into the real world. I found I had indeed been crying in my sleep. The pillow was wet with my tears. I tried to go back and sleep again to continue my life in that beautiful dream, but I could not.

For a long time I remained awake that night. It was perhaps a sign that the place of my birth (Kashmir) and Mother India would possibly see a bright and healthy future. I remembered some recent reports from Kashmir, on the occasion of *Herath* (Shivratri) this year, that many Kashmiri Muslims had cleaned several old Hindu shrines and temples in the valley. Maybe my dream was not totally unfounded! If there was anything I could pray for, that would be return of peace, harmony and prosperity to the Kashmir valley. It would herald a new, but everlasting, age of peace and prosperity in the history of Kashmir and India.

On a heart-warming note, I have come to know about a recent incident at Jammu. A well-known Kashmiri Pandit physician stumbled and fell down while crossing a busy road. He received injuries on the face and other parts of the body. A passing motorist recognised him and stopped immediately to help. Thereafter, he supported him in standing up and then took him to the nearest hospital for receiving immediate medical aid. That motorist happened to be a Kashmiri Muslim, on a short visit to Jammu. It also turned out that he had previously been the doctor's patient. Humanism, such as this, transcends other shallow man-made silos. After all, we are all humans first. Our other earthly identities are secondary.

Seventy years ago, in 1947, Bapu[53], the Father of the Nation, had seen a ray of hope in Kashmir, which he considered so vital for peace in India. The country was witnessing an unprecedented degree of volatility and uncertainty at that time, with Indians bleeding one another. What a waste and a tragedy! At that time, Kashmir held her nerve, thankfully! Holistically, 70 years later, though I have been living mostly away from Kashmir and India, I do actually see how and why Bapu saw that ray of hope, and why was that ray of hope so important for the country. It is not hard to see the importance of peace and well being of people living in Kashmir, if we see India as our Mother India.

After their separation, in 1947, the two portions of a united erstwhile India fought a number of major wars with each other. Now, they have their nukes aimed at each other! It does not matter who has more nukes, or who fires the first one—what matters is that after that first nuke is launched, it won't take more than a few minutes for both parts to obliterate themselves from the earth. It is a disappointment to see that a major portion of their respective budgets goes towards their defence, i.e. in the preparedness for war against each other. How illogical it sounds that these two countries must spend a predominant portion of their wealth in looking after their respective war machinery when both countries could be deemed as poor in so far as their 'per capita GDP' is concerned and that a significant portion of population in both countries could be deemed as poor by any yardstick. Is that what the founders of these two nations had conceived or planned? Then why should one country be afraid of the other? Why can't they recognise and respect each other's existence? Why can't they share their

---

[53] Means 'father' in the Hindi language. This is how people in India called Mahatma Gandhi, with love and reverence.

resources, both human and natural, for their common good and to achieve greater prosperity, not for making their politicians richer and more powerful, or for making their rich people richer, but mainly for the upliftment of their poor[54] masses, which comprise nearly half of their respective populations?

---

54 An online Pakistani newspaper, *The International News*, published an article on 3 June 2016, titled "Pakistan and India have identical poverty levels now'.
The paper reported, "*For the first time in the eventful post-1947 history of the Indo-Pak subcontinent, the poverty levels in both Pakistan and India are now resting at an identical yet alarming 29.5 per cent level, meaning thereby that every third Pakistani and Indian is literally fighting every hour just to beat hunger and looming starvation*", based on an economic survey in Pakistan and a CNN report, dated 3 August 2015, that had quoted Indian Planning Commission's estimates that 363 million citizens of world's largest democracy, making up 29.5 per cent of the total population, were living below the subsistence levels.
The newspaper added, "*The combined poverty figures of Pakistan and India signify that over 400 million Pakistanis and Indians are only striving today to earn a few loaves of bread and to breathe.*
In 2012, the Reserve Bank of India had stated 21.92 percent of the country's population was below its official poverty limit and in 2010, the CIA World Fact-book had calculated that the country's poverty level was resting at 29.8 per cent.
According to United Nation's Millennium Development Goal Programme, over 270 million or 21.9 per cent people, out of 1.2 billion of Indians, were living below poverty line of $1.25 in 2011-2012. In 2011, the World Bank had estimated that 23.6 percent of Indian population or about 276 million people were living below $1.25 per day on purchasing power parity. It is imperative to note that since 2005, Indian government had adopted the "Tendulkar Methodology," which moved away from calorie anchor to a basket of goods and had used rural, urban and regional minimum expenditure per capita necessary to survive.
In Pakistan, it is still not clear how the government has accurately calculated the national poverty level in absence of a fresh census. By the way, more than a million Indians are millionaires, yet most of their compatriots live on less than two dollars a day.
India was ranked fifth in the Knight Frank's Wealth Report 2013 with the highest net-worth individuals. As of December 2013, India had 122 billionaires with net assets worth Indian rupees five billion and above.
As far as Pakistan is concerned, the finance minister revealed publicly on Thursday that an amount ranging between $65 billion and $200 billion was parked by affluent Pakistanis in the secret vaults of the Swiss banks."

With these thoughts, I must have finally fallen asleep again that night and perhaps slept peacefully for a few hours, possibly under the spell of that beautiful dream in Kashmir.

As for myself, I am well settled outside Kashmir, with no plans or any desire to go and settle back in the valley. Similar could be the position of many of my fellow Kashmiris who also had to leave Kashmir under duress in 1990. But I certainly want to see myself in a position where I have the inherent human freedom of thought and action, as a son of the soil, and the availability of opportunities, to be able to go back to the valley and live a secure life there, as my ancestors did, without any undue concern for my honour, respect, dignity or personal safety.

5.2 A NIGHTMARE

That first night in Delhi, in March 2017, around the wee hours of the morning, I landed inadvertently in another dream world, which was entirely different in character to the earlier one. Actually, I must call it a nightmare. It was frightening. The scene seemed to be set sometime in the future, perhaps 2050. I saw myself in my eighties, frail and coughing. It seemed I had just landed from Australia and was on my way to Jammu to see my father. The arrival lounge appeared to be teeming with people and, because of the crowd size, it looked too small to hold that crowd and, therefore, seemed to be choking. It was not very easy for me to move through the crowd and to find my way out of the terminal building. As a matter of fact, I was pushed out of the main door by a large group of people who seemed to be in a great rush to leave the building, just like people coming out of a Mumbai train in the peak hour rush. Luckily, I was not run over, thanks to my resilience and endurance, due to the Australian lifestyle and a cleaner environment.

As soon I found myself outside the building, I observed chaos all around me. Many taxi drivers approached me to offer their taxis, which overwhelmed me. I could not initially decide with whom to go but then found myself walking with one who looked relatively a little older and frail. On the way to the taxi, he kept coughing. I stopped him and asked him if he was well and if he could drive. He said he was okay and the cough was a part of his life. He walked slowly.

I asked him how old he was. To my astonishment and shock, he said he was 45. From his behaviour and appearance, he actually looked not less than 70. I looked around and found many people wore ordinary dust masks while some wore gas masks. Some people, who looked richer by their appearance and clothing, carried a mini version of an oxygen cylinder at their back, just like underwater divers. Most people were bald, though some had tufts of grey hair. People looked much darker in appearance, as if they had been exposed to high levels of dust, smoke and toxic fumes. No one smiled and no one looked happy, as if they were zombies.

Slowly walking with my 'young' taxi driver, we finally reached his taxi. It was a small, two-seater taxi—and looked much smaller than a Tata Nano. I asked him what had happened to the regular four or five seater taxis. He said, "India has stopped manufacturing those large cars. There are no open roads to move, so we travel through narrow lanes. Also, the fuel is so expensive."

Life on the road looked very chaotic, with a lot of mixed traffic—pedestrians, cows, dogs, bicycles, two-wheeler motorcycles and scooters, two-seater cars and buses. Everyone seemed to be on a mission and looked serious.

Many pedestrians and drivers wore masks of one kind or the other. The traffic moved at not more than the speed of a common bicyclist, as there was not much space to move and surge ahead.

I asked my driver if he had a family. He said he had a wife but they had no children. He said they could not afford a child as both he and his wife were not keeping good health and it was so hard to make ends meet. Also, the child mortality rate and disease was very high because all local food was adulterated. A strong mafia was active across the country, busy in stealing healthy children.

Outside the car, when I looked above I could not see the sky. It was as if we were moving slowly through a fog, or actually smog. Visibility was not more than 25 m or so. I asked him why it was so foggy outside, and he said that it was the normal 'weather' in Delhi.

I asked my driver how people could live in that environment. He said only the poor people were left in the cities and the plains of India, as most richer people had either left the country or moved to the hills. But, even hilly weather had started catching up with the plains of India. Large scale deforestation across India had been accompanying mushrooming hillside developments, causing massive landslides every now and then, and cloudbursts. The country was struggling to keep up with the effects of a prolonged drought, or from the effects of frequent cloudbursts and sudden floods which was the reason for very high dust content in the atmosphere..

Most agricultural land had been transformed into residential and commercial developments. Most of the rivers had silted and dried up. Many lakes had been reclaimed and filled up to make land for commercial developments. The erstwhile Dal Lake in Kashmir was now a launch pad of satellite launches and space missions. Most of the richer people consumed imported bottled water and tinned food. Others consumed local, adulterated, food.

He seemed to be so well informed and knew so much about the country, so I asked him if he was educated. He said he had a doctorate in civil engineering.

Out of curiosity and a new found greater respect for a fellow civil engineer, I said, "I am sorry. We have been talking for quite some time now and I have not even addressed you by your name." Extending my hand, I said, "You may call me Bill. What is your name?"

He held my hand tightly and smiled, "You may call me B."

Out of added curiosity, I asked, "Thank you, B, nice to meet with you. By the way, what is your full name?"

He smiled and replied, "Well, that is my full name. These days people get targeted because of their religion and caste. Therefore, people are shy of getting identified with any religion or caste. I don't want to bring harm to myself; you may not like me based on my religious or caste background." I was left shocked and speechless. Before I could utter another word, he smiled and asked, "Isn't that the reason why you have also chosen to be called just Bill, and not your original Indian name?" With that shock, I woke up suddenly into the real world, with my heart pounding fast. It was about 7 am when I woke up; the sun was already up. I must have gone through a nightmare. There was still just enough time to prevent this from happening, but these ground issues had to be dealt with now. The real world was not so bad; I could see the sun still smiling at me through the window and the sky looked hazy and greyish blue.

That night I saw two dreams—very contrasting:

- The first one—a beautiful dream—was perhaps a result of my deep longing and a wishful thinking about return of eternal peace to my land of birth, Kashmir, and its flow-on positive effect on the rest of Mother India.
- The other one—a nightmare—was perhaps a result of my dreadful fear about how Indian cities may look in the future if population and its flow-on effects on life in India were not addressed in time as a top priority, without wasting any time on politics and the political correctness etc.

I am not very sure which one of these dreams will come true. It is up to the people of India to chart out the course of their future.

Chapter 6
Going Forward

6.0 RECOGNISE THERE ARE ISSUES

Acceptance of any issue is the start of a conscious recovery process required to find its solution, followed by the implementation of that solution.

Before any problem is addressed, it is important that one must first recognise and accept that there is a problem. A constant denial, or an ostrich-like attitude, or an escapist tendency to brush the problem under the carpet, and a proclamation that all is hunky-dory, knowing very well that a problem is looking straight into your face and you deliberately refuse to look at it, leads one to ignore it, invariably with sad and disastrous consequences. The end can be imagined similar to a situation when a hunter eventually catches up with a fleeing ostrich, with its head still buried in the sand, and grabs it from behind. How long can that ostrich run away from the hunter?

This book has been written for life—for living a good and healthy life; for living a happier life; for the good health of Mother India and all her children, young and old, existing, and the future children. And that life in India, as far as I can see is under an existential threat, due to a range of issues, some obvious and some not so obvious, and some due to quintessentially Indian culture and an outdated mindset, which may potentially have unfortunate and irreversible consequences if not addressed now in a timely manner, especially when we still have the time, thankfully, for the implementation of a broad range of preventive and recovery measures.

6.1 WHAT DOES LIVING A LIFE MEAN?

First, let us revisit the term 'life'. Does life mean becoming rich and famous, as most Indians aspire at the moment; or does it mean living in a large and lavish bungalow, owning expensive cars, surrounded by a retinue of servants? Or does life mean having to live with both internal joy and external comforts? Or does life mean just living every moment as it comes, and being with oneself and enjoying one's own company? To some, it may mean some of these; to others, it may mean none of these; while to some, it may mean all of these!

Let us try to answer the following basic questions that have challenged us human beings since our existence on the planet:

Why are we here? Where are we going? What is the purpose of our existence?

Answers to these questions are subjective and, as such, there is no conclusive answer. People try to answer these questions using their religious faith and philosophy about life, as many humans do not think deep enough. Most people remain busy with tasks that are important for their survival.

A healthy body is important for a healthy mind, and vice versa. For a healthy body, what do we need? A logical answer would be clean air and clean water, adequate food, appropriate clothing and an engaging activity. Now, what does a healthy mind mean? A logical answer would be a mind that is peaceful and settled.

In this world, especially in the modern India, most people believe the purpose of life is to achieve all materialistic success in order to be happy. It is the effect of a relative affluence, as many Indians are climbing a growing economy curve. For them, the route to happiness is through consumption of materialistic comforts. They constantly try to chase happiness by consuming whatever is available out there for consumption. They believe happiness lies in the external world. They fail to think deeply why so many famous and successful people across the world, after reaching the height of their materialistic success, long for something beyond accumulation of material wealth, power to exercise control over fellow human beings, and fame. These rich people, at some stage of life, search for their own self. They look for the source of joy within themselves.

Maharishi Mahesh Yogi[55] said, *"If you want to be in peace, radiate peace for others; make everyone happy; 'as you sow, so shall you reap' is the ultimate analysis—whosoever you may be ... at any time."* He also said, "*the happiness increases as the consciousness expands.*"

For a balanced life and to maximise the level of internal happiness and overall well-being of an individual and a nation, Maharishi also advised, "*Live life 200 percent,*" which means—100 percent material and 100 percent spiritual, like the two wheels of a bicycle. The spiritual activity of an individual imparts a more balanced dimension to that individual's material tendencies. A person is then empowered to make more use of his brain and critically assess the basic objectivity of consuming anything or engaging in any activity. With that settled state of mind, a consumer will ask himself, "*Why am I doing this, what is the purpose of this activity?*"

It is at that moment that a human being transcends all other animals on the earth. Otherwise, we are also breeding and consuming like them.

A forward looking, progressive, person must simplify and stop mindless consumption of material and natural resources. That ability to ask ourselves why we are doing any particular activity sets us apart from other animals.

---

[55] Maharishi Mahesh Yogi (12 January 1918–5 February 5 2008) developed and introduced the Transcendental Meditation technique (also known as 'TM') to the world in 1955.

On his 90th birthday, on 12 January 2008, about a month before he passed on, his farewell message to the world was: "It has been my pleasure at the feet of Guru Dev to take the light of Guru Dev and pass it on in my environment. Now today, I am closing my designed duty to Guru Dev. And I can only say, '*Live long the world in peace, happiness, prosperity and freedom from suffering.*'"

Maharishi maintained that the very nature of consciousness is blissful happiness and as we have more consciousness available to our experience, our happiness keeps growing naturally in a very spontaneous way. He said the nature of life itself is happiness and everyone seeks more happiness. He suggested that we tap our internal sources of happiness and focus on the expansion of our consciousness. To remain happy and fulfilled, therefore, one must lead a lifestyle which includes a spiritual activity, such as meditation, on a daily basis, and endeavour to find happiness through the state of our mind and consciousness, which is peaceful and energetic, and filled with love and contentment. Thereafter, we'll act in our daily lives with that peaceful, energetic and contented state of mind, charged with love.

When we are truly happy, small things that normally irritate us become insignificant because we are filled with happiness. We ignore and transcend all man-made divisions of religion, caste, class, ethnicity, gender etc. We tend to enjoy the external sources of happiness only when we are settled internally. Internal settlement and activation of internal source of joy is paramount to living a contented and happy life. If we lack internal happiness, it will be relatively hard for us to enjoy anything outside of us.

Therefore, internal happiness is the key to living a happy life. All we need to do is to remove the internal barriers that cause stresses and strains within us, and allow our nature to be what it is supposed to be in its pure and natural state, like a child's.

6.1.1 Liveability & Peace

For liveability of any place, the focus must be on the maintenance of high quality of life of its people.

For health and sustainability, clean air and clean drinking water are most important. People must exercise a high degree of frugality in the use of their natural resources. It is important that human pressure on all natural resources is minimised. That can happen if population is controlled and capped at a more sustainable and manageable level. Also, the people must take care of their environment and look after the ecology of their country.

For the sustainability of a place, sustainable peace amongst the people must be given paramount importance.

In a multicultural, multi-ethnic and multi-religious country like India, it is paramount that diverse ethnicity and religion of her people must never be allowed to divide her people and become a source of strife. Religion must be considered as a private affair of the individuals and never be allowed to be used for discrimination or marginalisation. People belonging to any one religion must not try to claim or enjoy superiority over people belonging to other religions, or impose their thoughts and values on others.

A predominant number of people (around 75% to 85%) in the ten most liveable cities of the world either practice various forms of Christianity or no particular religion at all. The remaining 15% to 25% are understood to collectively practice Judaism, Buddhism, Islam, Hinduism, Sikhism etc. Religious thoughts and values must be objectively tailored and effectively made compatible with the changing times to enable all youth to fit in seamlessly with their fellow citizens and the world community at large. If the religious values are not modified and adapted to the changing times, the degree of confusion, as well as the potential strife resulting therefrom, will potentially increase with each year that goes by, with violence becoming a normal affair.

Life goes forwards (and not backwards) and so does a civilisation. Therefore, in this world of globalisation, various religions should adapt to the demands of the changing times. Their followers should pray, care and work not only for themselves but equally also for all other people who don't follow their religion, without any fear, bias or discrimination. A religion that binds some people to the extent that they become incompatible and incoherent with the rest does not serve the peaceful demands of the fast changing times.

A religion should be used only to promote universal peace and brotherhood and, in no case, encourage any culture of hate and violence against humanity at large. The need of the hour is to dump and forsake all such outdated and irrelevant religious thoughts that alienate a community or an individual from the people that practice other religious beliefs or for that matter no religion at all. Importantly, religion should not be used for political reasons, especially in shaping the government policies.

6.1.2 Health of a Country

The health of a country is reflected in the health of citizens living in the country. People make a country. Therefore, when people are healthy, the country will be healthy. To achieve that state of health, people must invest in both physical and mental health; they should feed and support each other. Once people are healthy and happy, they will be able to think clearly and prioritise their activities and channelize their energies for achieving the greater good of themselves and the country as a whole.

Various notable medical researchers, philosophers and spiritual leaders have been shouting for a long time: *Don't limit yourself to yourself; expand and adopt the whole world as your body. If you are selfish by nature, then be selfish for the whole world and work for it. Focus on the world around you and endeavour to make it happy.*

Communal harmony is most important for national health and survival. People must transcend their religious and caste identities and work together. Every human being is unique; there is no need to compare one with the other. Nature did not use one mould to create all humans alike. No two trees, flowers, rivers, mountains are alike. People must accept one another as they are. For this to happen, they must be first happy inside.

The mantra is: *educate, educate & educate.* But first, be educated. India has a thriving parliamentary democracy, so force is not the answer. Mother India is known to have always nourished her children and all who came from outside and took refuge with her. She is kind and loving, and not cruel. India traditionally exemplifies a high level of tolerance and inter-communal harmony and brotherhood. India belongs to all people, irrespective of their religion, caste and gender. The famous BBC journalist, Michael Wood, in his 2007 BBC documentary series on India, *The Story of India*, called India as *Mother India* for all and not only for the present Indians.

Only through a prolonged and sustained educational campaign, led by the youth and the children of India, across the length and breadth of India, across cities and villages, through door-knocking and effective use of printed, electronic and social media, can an urgent awareness be raised in the masses of India that they must immediately review how they have been living traditionally and consuming the resources, because that is no longer sustainable. It will take a sustained, conscious, sincere and collective effort of all people in India, young and old, educated and illiterate, women and men, rich and poor to overcome the following white-anting issues identified in this book.

- Population growth: India must control her population growth and pull back the 'birth to death' ratio to one or less than one, as there is no other option left. A phenomenal population growth in India since her independence has had a detrimental effect on the overall level of happiness, well-being and the general lifestyle of her people, despite the fact they are living longer and are much more affluent.
  Sadly, the traditional Indian spirituality, which would produce a more balanced approach to life, has all but disappeared. It has become a rat race; but a rat race to what?
- Gender bias: How can a country progress when a substantial portion of her population does not enjoy parity with the other half? Women education and empowerment is essential for India to move into the future as a healthy country. Indians must undergo a complete shift in their orthodox and traditional, rather outdated, mindsets.
- Materialism and consumerism: An unbridled materialistic tendency seems to be feeding into all these issues. Indians must relearn to live simply and focus on the preservation of their natural resources. They must choose to be less greedy and consciously leave natural resources untouched for future generations. In doing so, they must understand they are only the temporary custodians of their land and her resources and can't afford to leave their country poorer with meagre resources for their future generations.
- Pollution: This issue is closely related to an uncontrolled population growth and a high consumption of fossil fuels. It is inconceivable that people can continue to live as they

are living now for long by breathing increasingly polluted air and drinking polluted water. Air and water pollution are continuously poisoning their bodies and brains.

- Ecological disasters: Deforestation and conversion of wetlands and agriculture lands into residential and commercial developments must be completely stopped. Pollution of water bodies, such as lakes and rivers must be immediately stopped. If wetlands and agriculture lands are consumed for human dwellings, how can the country grow enough food to meet the human demands?

  It is heartening to see that Uttarakhand High Court[56] has recently recognised River Ganga as the first living entity of India and granted her the legal rights equal to humans, which means, if someone pollutes the River Ganga, the law will see it akin to harming a human being. The court is reported to have said, '*The Ganga should be saved for the generations to come.*" Interestingly, a similar ruling was reportedly passed in New Zealand a week ago about Whanganui River.
- Adulteration: Like pollution, food adulteration is slowly but surely poisoning the bodies and the brains of the country.
- Rampant corruption: Like pollution and adulteration, this menace is also related to the population growth, which results in stiffer competition between people and the typical Indian psyche. Through proper education, people must be made to shift their focus from themselves onto their nation.

Once people enjoy good mental health, their approach to life will improve. They will be able to better manage all negative human emotions, such as anger, greed, jealousy, envy and selfishness. Once that happens, their family, social and professional lives will improve naturally and the country will become happier.

If we give a part of our self to our fellow citizens, through compassion, care and assistance, we achieve greater fulfilment in life. The system will take care of us and our needs. All people will grow at the same time. There will be no more rush, no rat race or fear of

[56] *The Hindustan Times*, dated 20 March 2017

losing anything. The country will be blessed when her people coexist and thrive peacefully and harmoniously.

"*Sab ka saath, sab ka vikaas*", as Mr Modi, the country's Prime Minister has said, which means "prosperity for all with everyone's support".

6.2 AN ENGINEER'S APPROACH

For risk assessment and hazard control on any engineering project, engineers go through the following process. Can this process be used to deal with India's ground issues?

- Step 1 Identify hazards, i.e. anything that may cause harm.
- Step 2 Decide who may be harmed, and how.
- Step 3 Assess the risks and take action.
- Step 4 Make a record of the findings.
- Step 5 Review the risk assessment.

In order of decreasing effectiveness, the following hierarchy in hazard controls is considered:

- Elimination–It is the most effective hazard control. It involves physically eliminating the hazard itself, e.g. removing a live electric cable from the road surface.
- Substitution–It involves replacing something that produces a hazard with something that does not produce a hazard.
- Engineering–Engineering controls isolate people from hazards but do not eliminate hazards, e.g. erecting a fence around a deep pothole.
- Administration–It means administrative changes to the way people work, including procedure changes, e.g. employee training, and installation of signs and warning messages.
- Personal Protective Equipment (PPE)–These include high-visibility clothing, hard hats, safety footwear, gloves, safety glasses and respirators. It is the least effective means of controlling hazards because of the likelihood of the damage to render the PPE itself ineffective.

Hierarchy of Hazard Control is a system used in the engineering industry to minimise or eliminate exposure to hazards and prevent or minimise work related injuries and, as a worst case scenario, human deaths. In the context of this book, India is seemingly left with no other options but to adopt one of the following approaches or a multi-faceted approach:

- **Elimination process to**
  - Check and stop the current unsustainable population growth.
  - Reduce and prevent environmental pollution and diseases due to polluted air and water.
  - Eradicate food adulteration practices.
  - Eradicate manufacture and sale of spurious and fake drugs and medicines.
  - Eradicate corrupt practices across the nation through numerous strata.
  - Eradicate traditional cultural gender bias against the women and female foeticide.
  - Break divisive societal divisions and silos.
- **Substitution process to**
  - Change the typical Indian mindset about consumerism.
  - Replace lavish weddings with simpler, less vulgar, cheaper, weddings.
  - Downsize the tall poppy syndrome by promoting dignity of labour, upholding inherent human dignity and promote equality amongst people, irrespective of their caste, creed, gender, religion, profession or wealth.
  - Promote healthy and appropriate food habits that suit people's lifestyle in 2017, so that diseases due to affluence and weight gain, such as Type 2 diabetes, hypertension, mental disorders, cancers etc., are prevented.
- **Engineering, Administration & PPE processes to**
  - Provide facilities to promote more active lifestyle in cities, such as walking, jogging and running tracks; cycle paths; parks and gardens.
  - Reduce traffic woes—by formal drivers' education, strict driving tests, implementation of standard international traffic rules, promoting alternative means of transportation based on use of cleaner energy; promoting use of seat belts

for all passengers in a car; promoting use of helmets for all two-wheeled vehicle users, including cycles.

- Address environmental issues—air, water, agriculture and forests.

Corporate India has played a major role in the current industrial and infrastructural development of India and, in the process, driven the country's economy. Corporate India has also, in turn, benefited and will undoubtedly continue to benefit from India's booming population, a fast growing economy, growing consumerism and affluence, and a marked shift from spirituality to materialism.

It is obvious the country is paying a high price, in terms of pollution, adulteration and corruption, for her development. Corporate India must take some responsibility for the current state of affairs in India and, therefore, be proactive in taking all necessary measures in alleviating the negative effects of their commendable work, which must include broader education of the masses, particularly the women in rural areas, use of cleaner energy, and uphold traditional values of India. Corporate India must, therefore, invest energy and resources to address, on a war footing, the various environmental issues in the country. Don't kill the goose that lays the golden eggs. Corporate India should be prudent enough to invest in the health and happiness of India's people in order to keep reaping benefits. They must adopt a '*win-win*' approach, with human happiness and well-being as the ultimate goal.

Instead of focussing on the established urban areas and cities, it would be prudent that, for undertaking further infrastructure developmental works in the country to shift the focus to rural and remote areas. Such a shift will potentially provide employment to the local people in or around their own villages and, therefore, reduce their tendency and need to move to urban areas and cities. Once that happens, pressure on cites due to an ongoing migration of people from rural to urban areas, will lessen. Assuming the population growth in the traditional city dwellers is possibly relatively lesser than village dwellers, the ongoing infrastructure in the cities should be able to catch up and cover the current needs of the city dwellers. Importantly, people would be able to breathe more freely and the city life would be more liveable. As this happens, the country will see a more uniform growth across the length and breadth of her land. And all her children will benefit.

Student union bodies, such as ABVP and NSUI, must join hands with each other, and with the government, in the greater interests of their nation, and embark on a serious nationwide campaign to raise a general awareness amongst the masses about numerous serious issues associated with a further population increase and, therefore, why there is an urgent need to curtail it. While doing so, they must also propagate important messages from the current government to the masses.

As for the general masses, they must strengthen the hands of their government and commit themselves to make their street, neighbourhood, suburb, city, state and the country safer and more liveable places to live.

A country comprises people, just like a human body comprises cells. Unless all people work in harmony and consciously towards the greater good of their country, they will not be able to secure their own future or the future of their future generations.

Delhi sits at the heart of India; that is also where the Central government sits. Who does not know how quickly sanitary and electrical fittings and fixtures corrode in Delhi homes and in millions of the homes within the surrounding areas of the national capital? If this corrosion can happen to the veins and arteries of our homes, imagine what must be happening to our own veins and arteries through the consumption of polluted and toxic water and air, adulterated food and spurious medicines?

To start with, without any fear or bias or any political correctness whatsoever, can the nation have an immediate, deep enough and wide enough national debate about what must be the maximum acceptable population of India? Just put a number on a piece of paper and start working backwards from there. In my opinion, the erstwhile governments should not have allowed the population to cross the 1 billion mark (100 crores), but that is another question. In no case whatsoever, the population must be allowed to exceed 1.35 billion, which is already one-third more than what it should ideally have been. However, there is no use crying over the spilt milk; let us work together now to save what is left.

The above question is akin to a question that we geotechnical engineers generally ask the structural engineer at the start of a geotechnical study—"What is the maximum loading that will be imposed on the ground by a structural column of a bridge or a building, and how much settlement can that column tolerate before the structure starts cracking and crumbling?" Note that we geotechnical engineers are responsible for the foundations of a structure, on which the overall stability of that structure depends. If foundations are not adequate—deep, wide and strong enough, the structure will undoubtedly collapse.

A national debate on the maximum population limit of the country is the call of the hour before it is too late. It needs a steely will and a concrete resolve. I am sure the country has enough of those tools and plants. It is only a matter of using that will and resolve. And that is what our Mother India is crying for. Can we please listen to her final cry?